TAKE
CHARGE
OF
YOUR LIFE

T0015362

BRIAN TRACY
TAKE CHARGE OF YOUR LIFE

12 MASTER SKILLS FOR SUCCESS

MEDIA

MEDIA

Published 2024 by Gildan Media LLC
aka G&D Media
www.GandDmedia.com

Front cover design by David Rheinhardt of Pyrographx

Interior design by Meghan Day Healey of Story Horse, LLC

Library of Congress Cataloging-in-Publication Data is available upon request

ISBN: 978-1-7225-0657-5

10   9   8   7   6   5   4   3   2   1

Contents

Twelve Master Skills for Success

1. Maximize your potential.
2. Understand the mental laws of the universe.
3. Employ strategic thinking.
4. Set meaningful and powerful goals.
5. Use the Twelve-Step process to revolutionize your life.
6. Tap into the power of the superconscious mind.
7. Master time management.
8. Streamline your life.
9. Increase your earning ability.
10. Find the career that you really want.
11. Use the power of leverage.
12. Achieve financial independence.

Introduction

This may be the most important book that you will ever read. It's taken me twenty-five years of reading and experience to put together the ideas you're about to read. They can save you many years of hard work and thousands of dollars in achieving the things you want in life.

To begin on a personal note, I started my life poor. My family never seemed to have enough money for anything. I did poorly in elementary school, and I failed in high school. When I went out on my own, the only job I could find was washing dishes in the kitchen of a small hotel. For several years, I drifted from job to job and city to city. Eventually I traveled from country to country, taking whatever work came along, and finally, working as a farm laborer.

When I was twenty-three, something happened to me, and I was never the same again: I realized that if I wanted my life to change, I would have to change. If I wanted my life to get better, I would personally have to get better. I saw that this life was not a rehearsal for something else. No one was coming to the rescue.

I began searching for the answer to the question, why are some people more successful than others? Why do some people make more money, wear better clothes, live in nicer houses, and drive better cars? I began asking for advice, reading books, listening to audios, and attending courses. I started selling. By studying sales at the same time, I went to the top of every sales organization I ever joined.

Then I got into management and began studying again. I enrolled in an MBA program at night school and eventually got a business degree. I learned about marketing, strategy, and negotiating in business development. I studied psychology, philosophy, and history. I learned about human potential and how to get more out of myself than ever before.

My situation gradually improved. I went from sleeping in my car to sleeping in my own house and then to a bigger house, and today, even a bigger house. I eventually went from rags to riches by practicing the things I'm going to share with you in this book. In 1981, I began teaching these ideas in seminars. From the very first one, people said that learning these ideas was like getting a brand-new chance at life, or a blank check on the future. I expanded the course and created other seminars. Later, I began making them available on audio and video.

In this book, I've put together the most comprehensive course on lifelong success ever created. I promise you that it will change your life.

Be sure to read this book more than once. As you do, stop and think about the key ideas you're learning. The teaching is in the words, but the learning is in the silence.

Now come with me, and let's journey to the frontiers of your mind and your infinite possibilities. Let's learn how you can fulfill your potential and become everything you're capable of becoming.

In the entire history of the human race, there never has been and never will be anyone just like you. You have the potential to do something extraordinary with your life—something that no one else can do. The only real question you have to answer is, are you going to do it?

Although some people are born with extraordinary gifts, most of us start off with talents and abilities that are more or less average. Most men and women who achieve great success do it by developing their natural talents and abilities to a very high degree in some special area. Your individual potential has to be nurtured, developed, and worked on if you're ever going to reach the point of getting something great out of yourself.

ONE

Maximize Your Potential

To achieve the success you desire, you have to develop and make use of your maximum potential.

One definition of individual potential is contained in the equation IA + AA x A = IHP.

The first two letters, IA, stand for "inborn attributes." These are what you're born with, your natural tendencies, your temperament, and your general mental ability. The next two letters, AA, stand for "acquired attributes." These are the knowledge, skill, talent, experience, and ability that you've gained or developed as you've grown. The third letter, A, stands for "attitude": the kind of mental energy that you bring to bear on your combination of inborn and acquired attributes. Finally, **IHP** stands for *individual human performance.* So the formula is, inborn attributes plus acquired attributes, multiplied by your attitude, equals your individual human performance. Since the quality and quantity of your attitude can be increased almost without limit, a person with average inborn attributes and average acquired attributes can still perform at a high level if he or she has a very positive mental attitude.

Attitude and Expectations

Your attitude, as much as or more than your aptitude, determines your performance. For this reason, the late inspirational speaker Earl Nightingale referred to *attitude* as the most important word in the English language.

Attitude is the most important word in the English language.

We know we should have a positive mental attitude, but what is it exactly? I would define *attitude* simply as *a way of responding to adversity and difficulty.* The only way that you can tell what kind of an attitude you really have is by observing how you react when things go wrong.

Your attitude in turn is determined by your expectations. If you expect things to go well, you'll have a generally positive attitude. If you believe that something wonderful is going to happen to you today, your attitude will be positive and optimistic. You'll be enthusiastic and primed for success.

Your expectations in turn are determined by your beliefs about yourself and your world. If you have a positive worldview, if you believe that the world is a pretty good place and you are a pretty good person, you'll tend to expect the best from yourself, from others, and from the situations you meet. Your positive expectations will be expressed as a positive mental attitude, and people will reflect back to you the attitude that you have expressed toward them.

Your values and beliefs largely determine the quality of your personality, but where do your beliefs come from? This brings us to perhaps the greatest breakthrough in twentieth-century psychology: the discovery of the self-concept.

Your Self-Concept

Your self-concept is your bundle of beliefs about yourself and about every part of your life and your world. It is the master program of your mental computer. Your beliefs determine your reality, because you always see the world through a screen of preconceptions and prejudices formed by those beliefs. For this reason, your self-concept, your belief structure, precedes and predicts your levels of performance and effectiveness in every area of your life. You always act in a manner consistent with your self-concept, consistent with a bundle of beliefs that you have acquired from infancy onward. There is a direct relationship between your level of effectiveness and your self-concept. You can never perform in any area at a higher or better level than your concept of your ability to perform.

Your self-concept is the master program of your mental computer.

Your self-concept is largely subjective: it's not based on fact but on impressions and information that you've taken in about yourself and accepted as true. In most cases where your self-concept in a particular area is low, it's based on erroneous data. It's based on self-limiting beliefs or false information that you've accepted as true.

Not only do you have an overall self-concept, which is a summary statement of all your beliefs about yourself, but you also have a series of many self-concepts, which control your performance and behavior in each individual area of your life. For example, you have a self-concept for how much you weigh, how much you eat, how much you exercise, how fit you are, how you dress, and how you appear to other people. You have a self-concept of yourself as a parent and as a child to your parents.

You have a self-concept for how popular you are among your social circles. You have a self-concept of how well you play each sport, and even for how well you play each part of each sport. For example, a golfer may have a self-concept as a great driver and another self-concept as a poor putter. If you're in sales, you have a self-concept of how good you are as a salesperson overall, but you will also have other self-concepts about how good you are at prospecting, answering objections, and closing. You have a self-concept of your own time management, organization, and efficiency in both your personal and your work life. You'll always perform in a manner consistent with these self-concepts.

Self-Concept and Money

You also have a self-concept for how much money you're capable of earning. You can never earn much more or less than your self-concept of your level of income. If you earn more than 10 percent above or below what you feel you are worth, you immediately begin engaging in compensatory behaviors. If you earn 10 percent too much, you begin to spend the money, lend it, invest it in things that you know nothing about, and even give it away or lose it. These throwaway behaviors occur to anyone who suddenly finds himself or herself with more money than is consistent with his or her self-concept.

Countless scores of men and women have won large sums of money in lotteries. In most cases, if they were working at laboring jobs when they won, in two or three years they are back working at the same jobs. Their money is gone, and they have no idea where it went.

On the other hand, if you earn 10 percent or more below your self-concept of your level of income, you begin to engage in scrambling behaviors. You begin to think more creatively to work longer and harder. You look at second-income opportunities or think about changing jobs in order to get your income back up into your self-concept range.

Your self-concept level of income is called your *comfort zone*. According to one study, it is about 40 percent below what the average person really feels he or she needs and would like to earn. Where money is concerned, people struggle to get into their comfort zones, and once they get there, they do everything possible to resist anything that would move them out. This natural tendency to get stuck in a comfort zone is called *homeostasis*: a striving for constancy and consistency.

Your comfort zone is the great enemy of your individual potential. Because of it, human beings tend to resist any change, even positive change, that would force them to leave their comfort zones. Your comfort zone soon becomes a habit, and your habits eventually become ruts. Then, instead of using your intelligence and creativity to get out of your ruts, you use most of your mental abilities trying to make your rut more comfortable by justifying and rationalizing your situation.

Your comfort zone is the great enemy of your individual potential.

Fortunately, you can increase your income by systematically jacking up your self-concept. Once you learn how to do this, as you will later on in this book, you'll be able to increase your income 25–50 percent per year for as long as you want.

The Self-Ideal

Your self-concept is made up of three parts. The first is your *self-ideal*. This is the vision or description of the person that you would most like to be in every respect. This ideal or vision of your possible future exerts a powerful influence on your behavior and on the way you think of yourself. This ideal is made up of a combination of all the qualities and attributes that you admire in yourself and in other people, living and dead.

High-performing men and women have very clear self-ideals toward which they're constantly striving. The clearer you are about the person you want to become, the more likely it is that day by day, you will evolve into that person. You will rise to the height of what you most admire, to your dominant aspirations.

By contrast, unsuccessful and unhappy men and women have only a very fuzzy self-ideal, or in most cases, none at all. They give little or no thought to the person they want to be or to the qualities they would like to develop in themselves. Consequently, their growth and evolution eventually slow down and stop. They get stuck in a mental rut, and they stay there. They don't change or improve.

The Self-Image

The second part of your self-concept is your *self-image*. Your self-image is the way you see yourself in your mind's eye and the way you think about yourself, minute by minute, as you go about your daily activities. Your self-image is often called your "inner mirror," into which you look to see how you're supposed to act in a particular situation. You always perform on the outside in a way that consistent with the picture that you hold of yourself on the inside.

Fortunately, you can dramatically improve your performance by systematically changing the pictures that you hold about yourself.

Self-Esteem

The third part of your self-concept is your *self-esteem*: how you feel about yourself. It's the emotional component of your personality, and it is the foundation quality of high performance, happiness, and personal effectiveness. It's like the reactor core of a nuclear power plant. It's the source of the energy, enthusiasm, vitality, and optimism that power your personality and make you into a high-achieving man or woman.

Your level of self-esteem is determined by how valuable and worthwhile you feel on the one hand and how competent and capable you feel on the other. Each reinforces the other. When you feel good about yourself, you perform well. When you perform well, you feel good about yourself. The best definition of self-esteem is how much you like yourself.

The more you like yourself, the better you do at everything you put your mind to. The more you like yourself, the more confidence you have. The more positive your attitude, the healthier and more energetic you are and the happier you are overall. Men and women with high self-esteem tend to be peak performers and high achievers in their work and personal relationships.

You can raise your self-esteem at will by simply repeating, with enthusiasm and conviction, *"I like myself, I like myself, I like myself."* If you do this, your self-esteem goes up, and your ability to perform and your level of effectiveness in every area of your life go up simultaneously.

Some people have been taught to believe that liking yourself is the same as being conceited or arrogant, overbearing, or obnoxious.

On the contrary, these negative behaviors are really a manifestation of low self-esteem, of not liking oneself very much at all.

Here are two rules regarding self-esteem and self-liking: (1) You can never like or love anyone else more than you like or love yourself. You can't give away what you don't have. (2) You can never expect anyone else to like or love you more than you like, love, or respect yourself.

Your own level of self-liking and self-esteem is the control valve on the quality of your human relationships. It's either the problem or the solution to every situation. Everything you do to build and reinforce your level of self-esteem will improve and increase your level of satisfaction, your effectiveness, and your happiness.

Origins of the Self-Concept

Where does the self-concept come from? We know that we all have one, but where does it originate?

No one is born with a self-concept. Everything that you know and believe about yourself today, you have learned as the result of what has happened to you since you were an infant. Each child comes into the world as pure potential, with a particular temperament and certain inborn attributes, but with no self-concept at all. Every attitude, behavior, value, opinion, belief, and fear has been learned. Therefore, if there are elements of your self-concept that don't serve your purposes, they can be unlearned, as I'll explain later.

An example of this ability to unlearn an old self-concept and relearn a new one is contained in a story that appeared recently about a thirty-two-year-old woman who was involved in an automobile accident. As a result of hitting her head, she experienced total amnesia. At the time of the accident, she was married with two children, eight and ten years old. She was extremely shy. She had a stutter, and she was very nervous around other people. She had a poor self-concept and a low level of self-esteem; to compound this problem, she didn't work, and she had a very limited social circle.

Because this woman had total amnesia, when she woke up in the hospital, she didn't remember a single thing about her past life. She didn't remember her parents. She didn't remember her husband or her children. Her mind was a complete blank. This was so unusual that several specialists were called in to examine her. It was such an extraordinary case that she became very well known.

When this woman recovered her physical health, she was interviewed on radio and television. She started studying her condition and eventually wrote articles and a book describing her experience. Then she began traveling and giving lectures to medical and professional groups. Ultimately, she became a recognized authority on amnesia.

With no memory of her previous reinforcement history, her childhood, or her upbringing, and as the result of being the center of attention and being treated as an important person, this woman developed a totally new personality. She became positive, self-confident, and outgoing. She became gregarious and extremely friendly, developing a tremendous sense of humor. She became popular and moved in an entirely new social circle. In effect, she developed a brand-new self-concept that was completely consistent with high performance, happiness, and life satisfaction.

You can do the same. Once you understand how your self-concept was formed, it'll be possible for you to bring about changes that make you into the kind of person you admire and want to be like; the kind of person who can accomplish the goals and dreams that are important to you.

As I said before, a child is born with no self-concept. Children learn who and how important they are by the way they are treated from infancy onward. The foundation of adult personality is laid down in the first three to five years. The health of the developing child's personality will be largely determined by the quality and quantity of unbroken love and affection that the child receives from the parents during this time.

The infant has a tremendous need for love and touching. In fact, you can't give a child too much love and affection during the formative years. Children need love almost as much as they need food, drink, and shelter. A child who's raised with love, warmth, affection, and encouragement will tend to develop a positive and stable personality early in life. A child who is raised with criticism and punishment will tend to grow up fearful, suspicious, and distrustful, with the potential for many personality problems that may manifest themselves later in life, like low self-esteem or a negative mental attitude.

Children are born with two remarkable qualities. The first is that they are born largely unafraid. Children are born with only two physical fears: the fear of loud noises and the fear of falling. All other fears have to be taught through repetition and reinforcement as the child is growing up. Anyone who's ever tried to raise a small child to the age of five or six knows that they are not afraid of anything. They will climb up on ladders, run out into traffic, grab sharp instruments, and do other things that appear suicidal to the adult. This is because they have no fears at all until those fears are instilled in them by their parents and others.

The second remarkable quality of children is that they're completely uninhibited. They laugh, they cry, they wet themselves, they say and do exactly what they feel like, with no concern whatsoever for the opinion of others. They're completely spontaneous and express themselves easily and naturally, with no inhibitions at all. Have you ever seen a self-conscious baby?

This is everyone's natural state. It's the way we come into the world, unafraid and uninhibited, completely fearless and able to express ourselves easily in all situations. You probably will have noticed that as an adult, whenever you're in a safe situation with people that you trust, you often revert to this natural state of fearlessness and spontaneity. You feel loose and at ease. You feel free to be yourself. You also recognize that these are some of the best moments of your life. These are your peak experiences.

Learning, Positive and Negative

During their formative years, children learn in two ways.

First, they learn by imitation of one or both parents. Many of our adult habit patterns, including our values, attitudes, beliefs, and behaviors, were formed by observing our parents when we were growing up. The sayings, "Like father, like son" and "Like mother, like daughter," are certainly true. Often the child will identify strongly with one parent and will be more influenced by that parent than by the other.

The second way children learn is by moving away from discomfort toward comfort, or away from pain toward pleasure. Sigmund Freud called this the *pleasure principle*, and he said it was the basic motivation for all human behavior. Children's behavior, from toilet training to eating habits, is shaped by this continual movement toward comfort or pleasure and away from pain or discomfort.

Of all the discomforts that can affect a child's behavior, the withdrawal of the love and approval of the parent is the most traumatic. Children have an intense ongoing need for their parents' love, support, and encouragement. When the parent withdraws love in an attempt to discipline or control the child, the child becomes extremely uncomfortable and even frightened. The child's perception is everything. When children perceive that love has been withdrawn, they immediately begin to change their behavior in order to win back the parent's love and approval. Without a continuous and unbroken flow of unconditional love, the child's need for security is frustrated, and his or her fearlessness and spontaneity become lost.

One psychologist said that all personality problems are the result of love withheld. Probably everything that we do in life from childhood onward is either to get love or to compensate for the lack of love. Most of our unhappy memories of childhood are associated with the perceived lack of love from our parents.

All personality problems are the result of love withheld.

At an early age, as a result of the mistakes parents make in raising their children—especially the use of destructive criticism and physical punishment—children begin to lose their natural fearlessness and spontaneity and develop negative habit patterns. A habit, positive or negative, is a conditioned response to stimuli. It's learned as the result of repetition over and over until it's firmly ingrained in the subconscious mind, where it takes on a power of its own.

Inhibition and Compulsion

The two main negative habit patterns that we all learn in childhood are called the *inhibitive* and the *compulsive*. All negative habit patterns are manifested in the physical body. When you're in the grip of a negative habit pattern, you feel and react exactly as though you are in danger of physical harm.

The inhibitive pattern is learned when the child is told over and over, "Don't; get away from that. Stop that, don't touch, watch out." The child's natural impulse is to touch, taste, smell, feel, and explore every part of his or her world. But when the parents react to the child's actions by shouting, becoming upset, or spanking the child, the child doesn't understand. Instead, the child internalizes the message: "Every time I try something new or different, Mommy or Daddy gets mad at me and stops loving me. It must be because I'm too small. I'm incompetent, I'm incapable. I'm stupid. I can't. I can't. I can't."

This feeling that "I can't" soon crystallizes into the fear of failure, and the fear of failure is the greatest single obstacle to success in adult life. The fear of failure paralyzes us whenever we think of taking any kind of a risk or doing anything new or different that might involve the loss of time, money, or emotion.

The inhibitive habit pattern is experienced down the front of the body, starting in the solar plexus, so for example, if you're afraid of public speaking and you are told that you're going to be called up in front of a large audience, your first reaction will be a feeling of fright—a tightening in your solar plexus, the emotional center of your body. The more you think about the coming event, the more the fear will spread. Your heart will start beating faster. You will begin breathing more rapidly and with shallower breaths, your throat might go dry, and you might get a pounding in the front of your head like a migraine headache. Your bladder might also fill up, and you could have an irresistible urge to run to the bathroom. All these physical manifestations of a negative habit pattern are usually programmed into your subconscious mind before you reach the age of six.

All negative habit patterns are manifested in a state of anxiety and nervousness, accompanied by perspiration, heart palpitations, and emotional responses, such as irritation and impatience, and even angry outbursts.

The second negative habit pattern that children learn is the *compulsive*. The compulsive pattern is learned by the child when he or she is told repeatedly, "You'd better or else." The parents say, "If you don't do or stop doing something, you are in big trouble."

To the child, trouble with the parents always means the withdrawal of love and approval. When parents make their love conditional upon the child's performance or behavior, the child soon internalizes the message, "I am not loved, and therefore I am not safe until and unless I do what pleases my mommy and my daddy. Therefore, I have to do what pleases them. I have to do what makes them happy. I have to do what they want. I have to, I have to, I have to." This compulsive habit pattern, which develops from being a victim of conditional love, soon manifests itself in the fear of rejection. The fear of rejection is the second major reason for failure and underachievement in adult life.

A person who's been raised with conditional love tends to be overly concerned, if not obsessed, with the opinions of others, especially with those of his or her parents, spouse, or boss. The compulsive negative habit pattern is manifested physically down the back, especially as tension in the neck and shoulders and stabbing pains in the back muscles.

Compulsive behavior is caused by the child's feeling that he or she never got the quality and quantity of love needed from the parent. It usually stems from the relationship between the father and the son or the mother and the daughter. Women tend to manifest the fear of rejection through depression, withdrawal, physical symptoms, and psychosomatic disorders. For men, this unconscious striving for love from the father is often transferred in adult life to the boss in the workplace, manifesting itself as type A behavior: an obsessive over concern with getting the boss's approval. In extreme cases, this can cause a man to become obsessive about his work, even to the point of ruining his health and his family.

When my father died, I took it very badly, because I felt that I had never been able to get it right, that I had never done the things necessary to get his love and acceptance. For two years afterwards, I felt a great sense of loss and sadness. Then one evening, I took my mother out to dinner and shared my feelings with her. She told me that I had no reason to be sad or upset. She explained that my father hadn't withheld his love; because of his background and upbringing, he had never had the love to give in the first place. He had very little love for himself and therefore very little for his children, including me. She told me that there was nothing I could have done to get more love than I got. It just wasn't there to give.

I have found that most men who suffer from type A behavior are still trying to earn the love and respect of their fathers, but after my father died, I learned that whatever love you get or got from your father was all there was. There is nothing you could have done and nothing you can do now to change it. Once you understand and accept that, you can relax a little and get on with the rest of your life.

Fear: The Greatest Problem

The greatest problem of human life is fear. Fear robs us of happiness. Fear causes us to settle for far less than we're capable of. Fear is the root cause of negative emotions, unhappiness, and problems in human relationships.

The greatest problem of human life is fear.

The only good thing about fear is that it is learned and therefore can be unlearned. The fear of failure and the fear of rejection are learned responses, programmed into us prior to the age of six. These fears set the upper and lower limits of your comfort zone. On the low side, you do enough to avoid criticism or rejection; on the high side, you do enough to avoid risk or failure. Once you have established your comfort zone, you stay there to avoid any feeling of fear or anxiety.

Fortunately, you can unlearn these fears. You can consistently and persistently eradicate them from your nature and your personality, and once you do, everything you want becomes possible for you.

The opposite of fear is love, starting with self-love. There is an inverse or opposite relationship between self-esteem and fears of all kinds. The more you like yourself, the less you fear failure and rejection. The more you like yourself, the more willing you are to reach out and take the risks that will lead you on to success and happiness. That will propel you out of your comfort zone.

You can raise your self-esteem, overriding and weakening your fears, by repeating with emotion and conviction the powerful words, "I like myself, I like myself, I like myself," over and over. Start off by repeating, "I like myself" fifty or a hundred times per day until it locks into your subconscious. You'll soon be able to see and feel the difference in your self-confidence and your relationships with other people.

An Action Exercise

Here's a powerful action exercise. Finish the following sentence with as many answers as you can think of:

If I were totally unafraid of anything or anyone, what I would do differently in my life is . . .

When you write the answers that complete that sentence, you will learn two things. First, you will learn what a big role fear plays in your life. Second, you will glimpse all the wonderful things you'll be able to do once you have unlearned your fears and developed unshakable courage and self-confidence, as you will as you continue to read this book.

White Rabbits and Happiness?

Before you become a great success, first you have to accept complete responsibility for who you are and everything that you become. You must accept without reservation that you're where you are and what you are because of yourself. If you want things to change, you must change first. Your thoughts determine your life, and because you're always free to choose the contents of your conscious mind—your thoughts—you are always fully responsible for the consequences of what you think. Your thinking determines your attitude, your conduct, and your behavior, and these factors largely determine your success or failure.

You are conditioned from infancy to believe and accept that someone or something else is responsible for your life. When you're a child, your parents take care of everything: they provide you with food, clothing, shelter, education, recreation, money, medical attention, and whatever else you need. Through early childhood, you grow up in a cocoon, where you're entirely provided for by other people. You're not responsible for your food; it's just provided. You're not responsible for your clothes; someone else buys them for you. You're not even responsible for your basic education; you just go where you're told to go and do what you're told to do.

There's nothing wrong with this. It's normal and natural that our parents provide for us during our formative years. The great tragedy is that the majority of men and women come into adulthood with a conscious or unconscious expectation that somewhere, somehow, someone is still responsible for them. This failure to accept and embrace the fact that you are completely in charge of your own life is the source of most unhappiness and underachievement.

Your parents' job is to bring you into the world and raise you to the age of eighteen: the age of maturity as a fully responsible, self-reliant adult capable of making your own decisions. From this point onward (and sometimes earlier), you are in the driver's seat. You are the architect of your own destiny. From this moment onward, whether or not your parents have succeeded in raising you as a self-reliant individual, there's no looking back. Everything you are, everything you become, is now up to you.

In one of Tolstoy's short stories, he tells about children who are told that the secret of happiness is hidden in the backyard of their home. They will be able to find it and possess it forever, as long as they do *not* do one thing: while they're searching for the secret of happiness, they must not think about a white rabbit. Of course, each time the children go out to search for the secret, the harder they try not to think about a white rabbit, and the more they think about it. And of course they never do find the secret of happiness.

Everyone has a white rabbit, sometimes many. These are the excuses that you use to avoid setting clear goals and making total commitments to your success in life. You need to become a skilled thinker if you sincerely desire to fulfill your potential. Part of being a skilled thinker is to objectively analyze any mental blocks or excuses that could be holding you back and that you may be using as reasons for not making progress.

Some of the most popular white rabbits that people use today are self-limiting ideas such as, *I'm too young, I'm too old, I don't have any money, I don't have enough education, I have too many bills, I'm not ready yet, I can't do it because of my boss, my children, my parents,* or some other reason.

What are your personal white rabbits? What are your favorite excuses for not making the changes that you know are necessary? If you are going to achieve your goals and fulfill your dreams, your job is to go rabbit hunting. Root them out and run them down. Carefully analyze them to see if they have any validity.

Here's a simple test: ask yourself, is there anyone anywhere with my problem or limitation who has succeeded despite it? If the answer is yes, you know that your excuse is not a legitimate reason for not going ahead. Whatever one person has done, someone else can do. "Excusitis," or the inflammation of the excuse-making gland, is a disease that is invariably fatal to success.

The Power of Accepting Responsibility

The acceptance of complete responsibility—giving up all your excuse—is not easy. It's very difficult, and that's why most people never do it. It's like making a parachute jump for the first time: it's both scary and exhilarating. When you cast free from your excuses, you suddenly feel completely alone. However, in a few moments, you start to feel a rush of excitement, your heart starts pounding faster, and you feel remarkably happy and free.

In any case, you can never give responsibility away as an adult; the only thing you can give away is control. If you try to make someone or something else responsible, you end up giving away control over your life, but you still end up 100 percent responsible. Furthermore, you'll feel negative, angry, anxious, or depressed. Self-responsibility is a key quality of the fully mature, fully functioning, self-actualizing individual.

High performers take both the credit and the blame for everything that happens to them. Low performers take the credit only for their successes and blame their failure on bad luck, other people, or circumstances beyond their control. Successful men and women have a strong sense of internal accountability, which extends to their work and all of their relationships. Failures try to make others accountable.

High performers take both the credit and the blame for everything that happens to them.

Sometimes I ask my seminar audiences, "How many of you are self-employed?" Usually fewer than 20 percent of the audience raise their hands. I point out to them that this is a trick question: the biggest mistake you can ever make is to think that you work for anybody else but yourself. We are all self-employed, irrespective of who signs our paycheck.

You are the president of your own personal services corporation. You are in charge. You are the boss. The top 3 percent of people in every field see themselves as self-employed. When they speak of the company they work for, they use words like *we* and *our* and *us*. Low performers refer to the company as though it were something separate and apart from them, as though it were just a job with no other meaning or significance.

There's a direct relationship between how much responsibility you are willing to accept and how high you will rise in any organization of value. There's a direct relationship between your income, your status, your position, your prestige, your recognition, and the amount of responsibility you're willing to take on, without excuses, for achieving the goals and objectives of your organization.

If you were an employer and you had two people working for you—one who treated the company as though it belonged to him and another who treated it as just a job, a place to come from nine to five each day—which one would you be most likely to promote? Which one would you want to invest in? To which one would you give additional training? To which of the two would you give or create opportunities for advancement? I think the answer is obvious.

Your attitude towards self-responsibility is one of the most important statements about yourself and the kind of person you are. You can put everyone on a scale from high acceptance of responsibility all the way down to low acceptance of responsibility, or irresponsibility. A highly responsible person tends to be positive, optimistic, self-confident, self-reliant, and self-controlled.

A person at the other end of the spectrum, with an attitude of irresponsibility, tends to be negative, pessimistic, defeatist, and cynical, as well as aimless, fearful, unsure, and often neurotic and mentally unstable.

The controversial psychiatrist Thomas Szasz said that there is no such thing as mental illness; there are merely varying degrees of irresponsibility. Self-responsible individuals tend to be both extremely healthy and positive. Irresponsible individuals tend to be extremely unhealthy and negative.

Responsibility and Control

This consideration brings us to one of the most important discoveries in the history of human psychology: there is a direct relationship between how much responsibility you accept in any area of your life and how much control you feel in that area.

Moreover, there's a direct relationship between how much control you feel in any given area and how much freedom you feel you have in that area. Responsibility, control, and a sense of freedom or autonomy go hand in hand.

There's also a direct relationship between how much responsibility, control, and freedom you feel and how many positive emotions you enjoy at any given time. There's a one-to-one relationship between the amount of responsibility you accept and your positive mental attitude or happiness. At the lower end of the spectrum, a person with an attitude of irresponsibility feels a lack of control, partial or complete. They feel that they have no ability to make any difference in their life; they're controlled by external forces and other people. A feeling of lack of control leads to a feeling of lack of freedom. These qualities in turn lead to negative emotions.

Robber Emotions

Negative emotions are what I call *robber emotions*. They are the single sole greatest cause of unhappiness, underachievement, and failure. Negative emotions make us physically and mentally ill. They ruin our relationships and harm our careers. They cast a shadow over everything we do. The elimination of negative emotions is job number one for the man or woman who aspires to great success and achievement. Peace of mind is the highest human good, and peace of mind only exists in the absence of negative emotions.

When I began studying this subject some years ago, I was astonished to realize that virtually all our problems are rooted in negative emotions. It became evident to me that if you could find a way to eliminate negative emotions, your life would be wonderful. All the mental principles would begin to work in your favor, and you would accomplish more in a short time than the average person accomplishes in years. I also realized that the failure to eliminate negative emotions would undermine all your efforts and take much of the joy and pleasure from anything that you managed to accomplish. It would also cause all the mental principles to work against you and could bring you more grief and heartache than any external factor in your life. The elimination of negative emotions is therefore central to the achievement of all lasting health, happiness, success, and prosperity.

The breakthrough that changed my life was the discovery that negative emotions are completely unnecessary and unnatural. There is no need for negative emotions. They serve no good purpose. They are only harmful. They are the major reason why men and women fail to grow and evolve to higher levels of consciousness and character, and we don't have to have them at all if we consciously choose once and for all to get rid of them.

Probably like you, I'd always thought that negative emotions were a normal and natural part of being human. I thought that just as you have positive emotions, you have negative emotions, that they were a part of human nature, to be accepted as inevitable, just like the rain or the sunshine. Then I learned that no one is born with negative emotions. Every negative emotion that we experience as adults, we had to learn, starting in childhood, through a process of imitation, practice, repetition, and reinforcement. Since all negative emotions are learned, they can be unlearned, and we can be free of them. Many people in our seminars have a very hard time with this subject. They have experienced negative emotions for so long that they find it difficult to accept that negative emotions are completely unnecessary and can be eliminated.

Since all negative emotions are learned, they can be unlearned, and we can be free of them.

Of course, whatever you believe with feeling becomes your reality. If you absolutely believe that negative emotions are a necessary part of your life, then they certainly will be, and they'll remain so.

It's easy to prove that negative emotions serve no useful purpose. Let's look at some of the more easily identifiable negative emotions. They are, first, doubt and fear: two of the biggest killer emotions. There are also guilt and resentment, which tend to go around together like twins. Then there is envy, followed closely by jealousy, that great destroyer of happiness and relationships.

There are about fifty-four negative emotions in total, but they all eventually boil down to and are expressed in the form of anger. Anger is perhaps the worst of all the negative emotions. Anger is either inwardly expressed—that is, you make yourself sick—or outwardly expressed: you make others sick.

Have you ever been angry? How do you feel when you're angry? Don't you feel as though there's a huge black blanket thrown over your mind? You find that you cannot concentrate, that your mind becomes totally preoccupied with the object of your anger. You talk furiously to yourself. The longer your anger goes on, the more all-consuming it becomes, like a fire burning out of control. It can rob you of sleep, friends, and employment. It can cause you to behave irrationally and act in ways that make you feel ashamed.

Does anything good ever come out of a negative emotion? The answer is a definite no: negative emotions, tied to irresponsibility, serve no useful purpose at all. Why, then, do people experience so many negative emotions? Let's answer that by starting off with the reasons why negative emotions begin in the first place.

Causes of Negative Emotions

There are four main causes of negative emotions. The first is *justification*. Justification takes place when we explain to ourselves and others why we are entitled to this negative emotion, why we are entitled to feel angry or upset. You can begin to eliminate negative emotions simply by refusing to justify them. Refuse to allow yourself the luxury of creating reasons why you're entitled to feel as bad as you do.

Judging others leads to condemnation and the accompanying emotions of intolerance and anger. That's why the Bible says, "Judge not, that ye be not judged" (Matthew 7:1). Have you ever been driving along in traffic and been cut off by another driver? Do you notice how instantly angry you become, even though you have never seen the other driver before and the other driver has never seen you before? You react exactly as if that driver had carefully plotted your route in traffic and then waited to ambush you as you came driving innocently along. However, the instant that you stop telling yourself what a terrible driver that other person is and just laugh it off, your anger quickly disappears.

The second major cause of negative emotions is *identification*: taking things personally. You can only become angry about something to the degree to which you can identify with the situation and see it as harming you in some way. The minute that you stop taking things personally, the minute you begin to practice detachment or *disidentification*—standing back from the situation—your negative emotions begin to diminish. Superior men and women remain calm and unemotional much longer than the average person; they refuse to justify or get caught up in the heat of the moment. They refuse to take things personally, but instead look at them from the viewpoint of a detached observer. This gives them tremendous mental control and makes them extremely effective in dealing with crises.

The third major cause of negative emotions is *lack of consideration*. We tend to become angry when we feel that people are not giving us our just due, that people are not respecting or recognizing us as we feel we're entitled to. In a social situation, if someone is rude to us, slights us, or doesn't pay enough attention to us, our egos become hurt and angry and defensive. As a wise man once said, "You should not worry so much about what other people think of you, because if you knew how seldom they did, you would probably be insulted."

You can begin to starve your negative emotions right now by refusing to justify them or identify with them and by refusing to let the behavior of others toward you get under your skin.

The fastest way to eliminate negative emotions, virtually in an instant, is to go to the root cause. The astonishing fact is that 99 percent of your negative emotions depend for their existence on your ability to blame someone or something else for something you don't like. *Blaming* is the fourth and final cause of all negative emotions, and it lies at the root of almost all of them. The instant that you stop blaming and refuse to blame anyone or anything else, your negative emotions cease.

Here is a simple switch that you can use to short-circuit any negative emotion: the fact that the conscious mind can only hold one thought at a time, positive or negative, and you can deliberately choose that thought. Whenever you feel negative or angry for any reason, you can immediately cancel the thought that is causing the negative emotion by firmly saying, "I am responsible." This is the most powerful affirmation for mental control ever discovered: the words "I am responsible" instantly turn your mind from negative to positive. They enable you to assert complete control over your emotions and make them positive. They cause you to become calm and relaxed and see the situation with greater clarity. These three words put you in charge of yourself and make you much more capable of dealing with this situation effectively.

The words "I am responsible" instantly turn your mind from negative to positive.

Here's the critical factor: you can develop no further than you have up to this moment with your negative emotions intact. All personal progress requires the systematic elimination of negative emotions. It's not possible to evolve to higher levels of consciousness except to the degree to which you free yourself from your negative emotions. It's as if you are freeing yourself from the forces of gravity that are holding you in your current reality.

This acceptance of responsibility for eliminating negative emotions is not optional. It is mandatory. It's essential to your health, happiness, and effectiveness. The development of a positive mental attitude toward yourself and your life, characterized by the elimination of negative emotions, will enable you to start using your higher mental powers in ways that today you cannot imagine.

As an exercise in clearing your mind, pause for a moment and think over your entire life, past and present, and then systematically analyze every single memory or situation that causes you to feel negative in any way. Neutralize the negativity associated with the memory or circumstance by simply saying, "I am responsible. I am responsible. I am responsible."

The fact is that you are responsible. Whatever difficulty or problem you have as an adult, in most cases, you got yourself into it. You were free to choose. In most cases, you probably knew at the time that you shouldn't be doing it, but you went ahead anyway, so you are completely responsible for what happened, for the consequences of your decision.

Often people ask me, "Isn't accepting responsibility the same as accepting blame?" The answer to that is that responsibility always looks forward, to the future; blame always looks backward, for the person who's to be punished or condemned. Someone runs into your car at a stoplight. You are legally not at fault, but you are responsible for the way you react to the situation. You are responsible for your conduct and behavior. You can either respond by becoming angry, upset, and emotional, or you can respond by being mature, calm, and controlled. The choice is up to you, and everything is contained in your response, not the situation itself.

Obstacles to Responsibility

Usually when we talk about responsibility in these terms, almost everyone agrees that from this point forward, they're going to accept complete responsibility in their lives. At the same time, almost every single person who has attended our seminars has also admitted that there is at least one area in their past where they have no intention of taking responsibility. They say, "If you only knew what that other person did to me, you wouldn't ask me to accept responsibility."

Now I must tell you a critical truth: the existence of even one negative emotion in your conscious or subconscious mind is enough to sabotage all your chances for great success. Let me give you an example that illustrates this key point. Imagine that you have been given a brand-new Mercedes automobile from the factory, beautifully engineered and perfect in every respect.

There is only one problem, though, and you don't know about it. A mistake was made in assembling the brakes: one front brake is locked on and cannot be released. Now let's say that you decide to take your beautifully engineered machine for a drive. You get in, start the engine, shift it into gear, and step on the gas. Even if everything in this car was perfect except for that one locked brake, what would happen as you stepped on the gas? You would spin around that locked wheel. The car would go around and around. No matter how hard you stepped on the gas or twisted the wheel, you would simply go around in a circle.

Your world is full of people who are just like that new car. They may be intelligent, good-looking, and well-educated and may seem to have everything going for them, but their lives seem to go around in a circle. It's because they are holding on to at least one key area of their life where they are refusing to accept responsibility. I have seen men and women fifty years old who are still angry over something that happened to them in their childhood. This refusal to accept responsibility hurts their relationships with their spouses, children, coworkers, and friends. It manifests itself as a variety of psychosomatic illnesses, and in extreme cases, it can even lead to early death.

You Become What You Teach

There's a saying that you become what you teach. Once you've begun accepting responsibility for every part of your life, large or small, start encouraging your friends and associates to do the same thing. When people tell you about their problems and frustrations, empathize with them briefly and then remind them, "You are responsible."

You become what you teach.

Perhaps one of the kindest things you can do for a true friend is to put him back in touch with his own good sense by reminding him that he is responsible. When a person complains, simply say, "You are responsible. What are you going to do about it?" Don't worry about giving advice. Someone said that the propensity to give advice is universal, but it doesn't matter, because the propensity to ignore it is equally universal.

At one time, my wife, Barbara, wanted to be a guidance counselor and eventually a psychotherapist. She would spend many hours listening to her friends and counseling them as best she could. Whenever I was involved in one of these sessions, especially with friends and coworkers, I would avoid all the back-and-forth and simply cut to the core of the matter, saying, "Well, you are responsible. What are you going to do about it?"

My wife felt that this was too simplistic and that I was not giving due consideration to the complexities of the various situations. But she was astonished to see how many of these people, after endless counseling sessions, actually went out and got their acts together.

Now Barbara and I have a standing joke around the house. When Barbara has lunch with a friend who has a problem or has spoken with somebody who's having some kind of personal difficulty, I'll ask her what she told the person to do. She now replies by saying, "I just gave him or her the advice, you are responsible. What are you going to do about it?"

Start to become your own psychotherapist by reminding yourself over and over again, "I am responsible. I am responsible, I am responsible." Then give the same advice to others who have problems; just say, "You are responsible. What are you going to do about it?" Then let them get on with the rest of their lives, and you can get on with yours.

An Action Exercise

Here is an action exercise for you. Take a pad of paper and draw a line down the center. On the left side, make a list of every person or situation about which you harbor negative feelings. Number each one.

On the right side of the page, write out a series of sentences that begin with, "I am responsible for this because . . ." and complete this sentence.

Do this for each item, and be as hard on yourself as you possibly can. Be brutally frank and honest. Write out every reason why you might be responsible for what happened. Do the same for every situation in your past or present that has caused negative emotions.

When you've completed this exercise, you'll be amazed at how much more positive and in control you feel. By saying, "I am responsible," your self-esteem goes up, and you move toward peak performance.

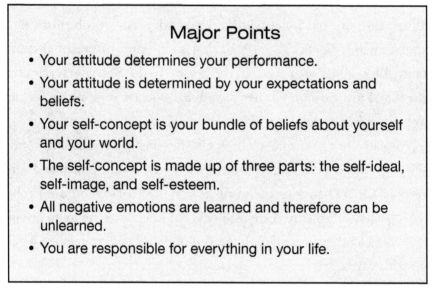

Major Points

- Your attitude determines your performance.
- Your attitude is determined by your expectations and beliefs.
- Your self-concept is your bundle of beliefs about yourself and your world.
- The self-concept is made up of three parts: the self-ideal, self-image, and self-esteem.
- All negative emotions are learned and therefore can be unlearned.
- You are responsible for everything in your life.

TWO

The Mental Laws of the Universe

From the earliest ages right up to the present, some of the finest minds that have ever lived have studied and written on success and happiness. There's more practical information available today on success than there ever has been at any time.

Yet even with all this wealth of information, only 5 percent of the population are financially independent at the end of their working lives. Fully 80 percent of people working today would rather be doing something else, and 84 percent of the employed population, by their own admission, feel that they are working below, if not far below, their potentials. Only 5 percent of men and women feel that they're producing at their full capacities in their jobs. In addition, more people are sick, overweight, unfit, and unhealthy than ever before. The United States spends more of its gross national product on health care than any other nation, and the costs are increasing.

America is a free society. All choices are open to the individual. People can do anything, be anything, go anywhere, change any part of their life for the better whenever they want. An enormous amount of illness is caused by negative mental attitudes and unhappiness. Why, then, do so many people persist in their negativity and pessimism when they're free to think anything they want? Why are so few people living up to their potential? I believe that the reason for much of this underachievement and frustration is simply that people do not know how to get the most out of themselves. They don't know how to operate themselves for maximum performance and happiness.

I'll give you an illustration. Imagine that someone gave you an expensive personal computer. It was delivered to your home, and when you opened it up, you found that there was only one thing missing: the instruction manual. Now imagine that you had no training at all in computers. You had to figure out how the computer worked, how to set it up, operate it, and get it to produce something of value. How long do you think it would take you, working without help or guidance, to figure out how to use a personal computer? Even if you were highly determined, it would probably take you years. Long before that, you would have turned your mind to other things and gone back to doing your work in the same old slow fashion.

Now let's imagine that you receive the same computer, but this time it came complete with an instruction manual that was user-friendly. In addition, a computer consultant came along and showed you step by step how to set up the computer, operate it, program it, and run it at maximum efficiency. You could have the computer up and running in an afternoon. From then on, you would get better and better at using it, and the quality and quantity of what you produced would rapidly increase.

The average person functions far below his or her potential because we come into this world with no instruction manual. We're born with an amazing brain, whose complexities and possibilities are so vast that we cannot yet understand or explain them. This marvelous three-pound organ contains around 171 billion cells and processes 100 million bits of information per hour. It maintains a perfect chemical balance in every one of the body's other billions of cells through the autonomic nervous system. Properly used, your powerful brain can take you from rags to riches, from loneliness to popularity, from sickness to health, and from depression to happiness and joy.

This book can be viewed as an instruction manual designed to help you get the most out of yourself by harnessing the amazing power of your mind to bring you anything you want. I will be your personal instructor, and I will show you how to do it. I will show you how to unlock your capacity for high achievement.

Natural Laws

There are two types of laws in the universe: man-made laws and natural laws. You can violate man-made laws, like traffic ordinances, and you may or may not get caught. But if you attempt to violate natural laws, you get caught every single time without exception.

These natural laws can in turn be divided into two categories: physical and mental. The operation of physical laws can be proven in controlled experiments and in the laboratory. Mental laws, however, can only be proven by experience and intuition and demonstrating their effectiveness in your own life. Some of the mental laws that you will learn in this book were written down as far back as 4,000 years ago. In the ancient world, these laws were only taught in the mystery schools. Students would enter these schools and undergo a period of training taking many years, during which they would be gradually introduced to these principles one at a time.

Mental laws can only be proven by experience, intuition, and demonstrating their effectiveness in your life.

In those days, these laws were never meant to be shared with the general public. The heads of these ancient schools felt that the average person would misunderstand and misuse them, and at that time they were probably right. Today most of these laws are discussed and written about quite openly, although only a tiny fraction of the population is even aware of them.

In studying the lives and stories of successful men and women, I found that almost all of them use these laws consciously or unconsciously. As a result, they were often able to accomplish more in two or three years than the average person accomplishes in a lifetime. In fact, all real and lasting success comes from organizing your life in harmony with these general principles.

Mental laws are like physical laws in that they are also in force 100 percent of the time. The law of gravity, for instance, works everywhere on planet earth twenty-four hours a day. If you jump from a ten-story building in downtown New York or downtown Tokyo, you will go splat on the sidewalk with equal force. It doesn't matter whether or not you know about gravity, whether or not you agree with the law gravity, or whether or not anyone ever told you about it when you were growing up. The law is no respecter of persons. To that extent, it's neutral. It works for you everywhere, regardless of whether you know about it or whether it's particularly convenient for you.

Although their physical effects can't be seen quite so easily, mental laws also work 100 percent of the time. Whenever your life is going great, it usually means that your thoughts and activities are aligned and in harmony with these invisible mental laws. Whenever you're having problems in your life, it's almost always because you have violated one or more of these laws, again, whether you know about them or not. You can always tell if you're violating them by the results you're getting, either positive or negative.

The Mental Laws of the Universe

The Law of Control
You feel positive about yourself to the degree to which you feel that you are in control of your own life. You feel negative about yourself to the degree to which you feel that you are *not* in control, or that you're controlled by some external influence.

The Law of Cause and Effect
For every effect, there is a specific cause. Everything happens for a reason. This is also called the *law of causality*.

A corollary is the *law of sowing and reaping*: whatever you are reaping today is the result of what you have sown in the past.

The Law of Belief
Whatever you believe with feeling or emotion becomes your reality.

The Law of Expectation
Whatever you expect with confidence becomes your own self-fulfilling prophecy.

The Law of Attraction
You inevitably attract into your life people and situations in harmony with your dominant thoughts. You have attracted to yourself everything that is in your life because of the person you are and because of your thoughts.

The Law of Correspondence
As within, so without. Your outer world reflects your inner world. You can tell what's going on inside you by looking at what is going on around you.

The Law of Mental Equivalency
Thoughts objectify themselves. Your thoughts, vividly imagined, repeated, and charged with emotion, become your reality. This is also called the *law of mind*.

The Law of Subconscious Activity
Any idea or goal accepted as true by the conscious mind will be accepted as a command by the subconscious mind, which will immediately go to work to bring it into reality.

The Law of Concentration
Whatever you dwell upon grows. The more you think about something, the more it becomes a part of your reality.

The Law of Substitution
The conscious mind can only hold one thought at a time, positive or negative. But the conscious mind is never empty; it's always thinking about something. As a result, you can substitute one thought for another.

The Law of Habit
Everything you are and everything you do is the result of habit. In the absence of a firm decision and determined effort on your part, you will continue doing and thinking the same things indefinitely.

The Law of Practice
Any thought or action that is repeated over and over again becomes a new habit.

The Law of Emotion
Human beings are 100 percent emotional: 100 percent of decisions are based on emotion.

The Law of Accumulation
Every great accomplishment is an accumulation of hundreds, even thousands, of hours and efforts that no one else sees or appreciates.

The Law of Reciprocity
If you do something nice for another individual, you will create within them an unconscious obligation or desire to pay you back and do something nice for you.

The Law of Compensation
A corollary of the law of sowing and reaping: for every action, there's an equal and opposite reaction. You will be compensated in kind for everything that you put in.

The Law of Overcompensation
The principle of doing more than one is paid for or expected to do.

The Law of Service
Your rewards will always be equal to the value of your service to others.

The Law of Return
You will get back in like measure to what you put in.

The Law of Superconscious Activity
Any thought, goal, plan, or idea held continuously in the conscious mind, whether positive or negative, must be brought into reality by the superconscious mind.

The Law of Control

The first of these laws is called the *law of control*. We have already discussed this to some degree.

The law of control simply says that you feel positive about yourself to the degree to which you feel you are in control of your own life. You feel negative about yourself to the degree to which you feel that you are *not* in control or that you're controlled by some external force, person, or influence.

You feel positive about yourself to the degree to which you feel you are in control of your life.

This principle is widely recognized in psychology, where it's called the *locus of control theory.* You can have an *external locus of control.* In this case, you feel helpless, like a victim, and unable to change some aspect of your life that's making you unhappy. You feel trapped.

It's generally agreed that most stress, anxiety, and tension and much psychosomatic illness come about as a result of feeling not in control of some important part of your life. If you feel controlled by your debts, your boss, your ill health, your bad relationship, or the behavior of others, then according to this law, you'll suffer a good deal of stress.

You can also have an *internal locus of control:* you feel that you are behind the wheel of your own life; you are the architect of your own destiny and the master of your own fate. Or you can have an external locus of control.

In every case, control begins with your thoughts—the only thing over which you do have complete control. How you think about any situation determines your feelings or emotions about it. Your feelings in turn determine your actions: what you do or refrain from doing in that situation.

Practicing self-discipline, self-mastery, and self-control begins with taking charge of your thinking. It begins with accepting that no situation can make you feel *anything*; it is only the way you think about a situation that can cause you to experience an emotion of any kind.

No situation can make you feel *anything*; it is only the way you think about a situation that can cause you to experience an emotion.

You can assert control of a situation in two basic ways.

First, you can take action. You can move forward and do something to change the situation. You can assert yourself in the situation and make it different somehow. Second, you can simply walk away. Sometimes this is the best thing to do in a situation where you feel out of control. If you've ever left an unpleasant relationship or quit an unhappy job, you'll remember how much better you felt when you stopped struggling with the situation. You felt back in control. You can also reassert control in a situation by letting it go and turning your mind to other things.

The Law of Cause and Effect

The second law is the *law of cause and effect*, the law of causality. It says that for every effect, there is a specific cause; everything happens for a reason. This has been called the iron law of the universe.

There are no accidents. We live in a universe governed strictly by law, and this is one of the most important of those laws. The law of cause and effect says that there are specific causes for success, and there are specific causes of failure. There are specific causes for health and illness. There are specific causes for happiness and unhappiness. If there's an effect in your life that you want more of, you merely need to trace it back to the causes and repeat those causes. If there's an effect in your life that you don't enjoy, you need to trace it back to the causes and get rid of them. A proverb says that it is better to light one weak candle than to curse the darkness. It is better by far to sit down and carefully analyze the reasons for your difficulties than to get upset and angry about them.

There are no accidents. We live in a universe governed strictly by law.

The Bible says, "Whatsoever a man soweth, that shall he also reap" (Galatians 6:7). We can call this the law of sowing and reaping. It says that whatever you're reaping today is the result of what you've sown in the past. If you wish to reap a different harvest in any area of your life in the future, you simply need to plant different seeds today. And of course this refers primarily to mental seeds.

The most important application of the law of cause and effect, or sowing and reaping, is this: thoughts are causes, and conditions are effects. Your thoughts are the causes of the conditions in your life. Everything in your experience has begun with a thought or thought— yours or others'. All causation is mental. Everything you are or ever will be is a result of the way you think. If you change the quality of your thinking, you'll change the quality of your life. Your outer experience will change in accordance with your inner experience.

The Law of Belief

The third law is the *law of belief*: whatever you believe with feeling or emotion becomes your reality.

The more intensely that you believe something to be true, the more likely it is that it will be true for you. Your beliefs tend to give you a form of tunnel vision: they edit out or ignore incoming information that is inconsistent with what you've decided to believe. The great philosopher and psychologist William James supported this concept when he said that belief creates the actual fact. The Bible says, "According to your faith, be it unto you" (Matthew 9:29).

To put it another way, you do not necessarily believe what you see, but you see what you already believe. If you absolutely believe that you are meant to be successful and happy in your endeavors, then no matter what happens, you will continue to press forward toward your goals. On the other hand, if you believe that success is a matter of luck or accident, you'll tend to become discouraged and disappointed whenever things don't work out for you.

People generally have one of two ways of looking at the world. The first is with a benevolent worldview. If you have a benevolent worldview, you generally believe that the world is a pretty good place in which to live. You tend to see the good in people and situations and to believe that there's plenty of opportunity around you and that you can take advantage of it. You believe that although you may not be perfect, you're a pretty good person overall.

The second way of looking at the world is with a malevolent worldview. People with a malevolent worldview have a generally negative and pessimistic attitude toward themselves and life. They believe that you can't fight City Hall, that the rich get richer and the poor get poorer, and that no matter how hard you work, you can't get ahead, because the deck is stacked against you. This type of person sees injustice, oppression, and misfortune everywhere. When things go wrong for them (as they usually do), they blame it on bad luck or bad people, so they are easily discouraged. They don't like or respect themselves very much.

People with a benevolent worldview tend to be the movers and shakers, the builders and creators of the future. They tend to be more optimistic and cheerful and to see the world as a better and brighter place. Their upbeat mental attitude enables them to respond positively and constructively to the inevitable ups and downs of day-to-day life. A key part of your journey towards success is the development and maintenance of this benevolent or positive worldview.

This brings us to some of the major roadblocks that you must overcome to become everything you're capable of becoming: your self-limiting beliefs. These are areas where you believe, consciously or unconsciously, that you are limited in some way. Perhaps you feel that you are limited in intelligence because you got average or mediocre grades in school. Perhaps you feel you are limited in creative capacity or in your ability to learn and remember. Or that you're not very outgoing, or smart about money. Some people feel that they can't lose weight, quit smoking, or be attractive to members of the opposite sex.

Whatever your belief, if you believe it strongly enough, it will become your reality. You will always tend to walk, talk, behave, and interact with others in a manner consistent with your beliefs.

Fortunately, most of your self-limiting beliefs are not based on reality at all. They are based on negative information that has been given to you or that you have internalized and accepted as true. Once you've accepted it as true, belief creates the fact. As Henry Ford said, if you believe that you can do a thing or if you believe you cannot, in either case, you are right.

Most of your self-limiting beliefs are not based on reality at all.

Immediately begin to identify any self-limiting beliefs that might be holding you back. Often your spouse or a trusted friend can help you identify self-limiting ideas and beliefs that you are unaware of.

Remember, these beliefs do just as much harm if you don't know about them as if you do.

The Law of Expectation

Law number four is the *law of expectation*. It says that whatever you expect with confidence becomes your own self-fulfilling prophecy.

To put it in another way, what you get in life is not necessarily what you want, but what you expect. Your expectations of people and situations exert a powerful, invisible influence that causes people to behave and situations to work out just as you expect them to. In a way, you're always acting as a fortune teller in your own life by the way you talk about how things are going to turn out. Successful men and women invariably have an attitude of confident, positive self-expectancy. They expect to be successful. They expect to be liked, to be happy, and they are seldom disappointed. Unsuccessful people tend to create a climate of expectations of cynicism, pessimism, and negativity that somehow causes situations to work out exactly as they expected.

In his book *Pygmalion in the Classroom*, Robert Rosenthal of Harvard University describes how the expectations of teachers have an enormous impact on their students' performance. He found that if students felt that they were expected to do well, they did much better than they otherwise would have.

There are four areas of expectations that have an impact on your life.

The first is the expectations of your parents. We are all unconsciously programmed to try to live up to or down to the expectations that our parents expressed of us when we were growing up. The need for the approval of our parents goes on even after they are no longer with us. If your parents expected you to do well and confidently, positively encouraged you to do your best and be your best, this will have had an enormous influence on the person you have become. If, as happens in many cases, your parents expressed negative expectations of you or no expectations at all, you may still be unconsciously saddled with the burden of trying not to disappoint them. In one study, 90 percent of prisoners interviewed by psychologists in the U.S. penal system reported that they had been told over and over again by their parents when they were growing up that "someday you're going to end up in jail." They said, "We didn't disappoint our parents; here we are."

The second area of expectations that affects your behavior is your boss's expectation of your performance. People who work under bosses with positive expectations are happier, perform better, and get more done than those who work under bosses who are negative or critical. Consciously and unconsciously, you need to be aware that you are inordinately influenced by the expectations of people whom you respect and who are important to you. That is why it's doubtful that you will ever be happy or successful working with or for people who operate in a climate of negative expectations.

The third area of expectations is your expectations of your children, your spouse, and your employees or staff. You have an enormous impact on the personality, behavior, and performance of the people who look up to you for guidance and feedback. The more important you are in the life of someone else, the more powerfully will your expectations affect their performance.

Perhaps the most consistently effective and predictable motivational behavior is to confidently and constantly expect the best from others. People generally try not to disappoint you. I always tell my children, "You're the best in the West." I tell them that I think they're wonderful children and that they're going to do great things with their lives. Does this have any impact? You'd better believe it. Try it yourself and see.

Many successful people attribute much of their advance in life to the influence of someone they respected who constantly expressed confidence in their ability to achieve. Perhaps the kindest thing that you can do for another person is to say, "I believe in you. I know you can do it."

The fourth area is your expectations of yourself. The wonderful thing is that you can manufacture your own. You can create your own mindset, your own way of confidently approaching the world, expecting the best of yourself in every situation. Your expectations of yourself are powerful enough to override any and all negative expectations that anybody might ever have had about you. You can create a force field of positive mental energy around yourself by confidently expecting to gain something from every situation.

Businessman and inspirational thinker W. Clement Stone was famous for being an inverse paranoid—someone who believes that the universe is conspiring to do him good. An inverse paranoid sees every situation as being heaven-sent to confer some benefit or teach some valuable lesson to help make him successful. This form of inverse paranoia is the foundation of a positive mental attitude. This is the most outwardly identifiable quality of a high-performing man or woman.

One of our seminar graduates who had been unemployed told me that he began saying to himself every morning, "I believe something wonderful is going to happen to me today." He repeated this over and over until he developed an expectant attitude that caused him to look forward to every event. Amazingly, a series of wonderful things did begin to happen to him. After being unemployed for six months, he received two job offers within the first week after beginning this exercise. His financial problems and legal difficulties miraculously seemed to clear themselves up. Wonderful things began to happen to him at every turn.

Just imagine if you went around all day believing that something wonderful was about to happen to you. Think how much more positive, optimistic, and cheerful you would be if you were absolutely convinced that everything was conspiring to make you happy and successful.

I can promise you this: if you try this exercise for three days, at the end of the third day, so many wonderful things will have happened to you that you will not be able to recount them all.

You can never rise any higher than your expectations of yourself. Since they're completely under your control, be sure that your expectations are consistent with what you want to happen. Guard them carefully. When you start consciously working with these mental laws, you have in your hands a power that is virtually unlimited. The power of positive expectations alone can change your whole personality and your whole life as well.

The Law of Attraction

The fifth law is the *law of attraction*. Many books have been written about this law, and many people feel that this law is central to understanding the human condition.

The law of attraction says that you are a living magnet and that you inevitably attract into your life people and situations in harmony with your dominant thoughts. You have attracted to yourself everything that is in your life because of the person you are and because of your thoughts. You have attracted your friends, family, relationships, job, problems, and opportunities because of your habitual way of thinking about these areas.

**You attract into your life people and situations
in harmony with your dominant thoughts.**

In music, this is called the principle of *sympathetic resonance*. For example, if you have two pianos in a large room, strike the note of C on one, and then walk across the room to the other piano, you will find that the string of C on the other piano is vibrating at the same rate as on the first piano. By the same token, you'll tend to meet and become involved with people in situations that are vibrating in harmony with your own dominant thoughts and emotions. All causation is mental. As you look at every aspect of your life, positive or negative, you must realize that your entire world is of your own making. In addition, the more emotion you attach to a thought, the more rapidly you attract people and situations in harmony with that thought into your life.

The law of attraction, like the other mental laws, is neutral. It can help you or hinder you. Actually, this law could be considered a subset of the law of cause and effect and sowing and reaping. That's why a philosopher said, "Sow a thought and you reap an act. Sow an act and you reap a habit. Sow a habit and you reap a character. Sow a character and you reap a destiny."

Thanks to the law of attraction, you can have more, be more, and do more, because you can change the person you are. You can change your dominant thoughts by exercising rigorous self-discipline and self-control and by keeping your thoughts on what you do want and off what you don't want.

The Law of Correspondence

The sixth mental law is the *law of correspondence*, which says, as within, so without. Your outer world reflects your inner world, and you can tell what's going on inside you by looking at what is going on around you.

The Bible expresses this principle when it says, "By their fruits ye shall know them" (Matthew 7:16). Everything in your life proceeds from the inner to the outer. Your external world of manifestation is merely an expression that corresponds with your internal world of thought and emotion. Your outer world of relationships will exactly correspond to your true inner personality. Your outer world of health will correspond to your inner attitudes of mind. Your outer world of income and financial achievement will exactly correspond to your inner world of preparation. The way people respond and react to you will correspond exactly with your attitude and behavior toward them.

Even the car you drive and the condition you keep it in will correspond to your state of mind at any given time. When you're feeling positive, confident, and in control of your life, your home, your car, and your workplace will tend to be well organized and efficient. When you feel overwhelmed with work or frustrated and unhappy, your car, your workplace, your home, even your closets will probably reflect this state of disarray and confusion. You can see the effects of this law of correspondence everywhere in your life.

The Law of Mental Equivalency

The seventh law is the *law of mental equivalency*. It can also be called the *law of mind*. It could actually be considered a summary of all the previous laws. Basically, it says that thoughts objectify themselves. Your thoughts, vividly imagined, repeated, and charged with emotion, become your reality.

Your thoughts become your reality.

Almost everything that you have in your life has been created by your own thinking, for better or for worse. Put another way, thoughts are things. The late inspirational speaker Earl Nightingale called it the "strangest secret": you become what you think about. Ernest Holmes, author of *The Science of Mind*, gave us another key when he said that if you change your thinking, you change your life.

Everything that happens in your life first takes place in the form of thought. Becoming a skilled thinker means using your mental powers in such a way that they will serve your best interests all of the time. When you choose to start thinking in a positive, confident way, you begin to exert and feel a sense of control. You sow positive causes and reap positive effects. You begin to believe in yourself and your possibilities. You tend to expect positive outcomes. You attract positive people and situations. Soon your outer life of results will begin to correspond to your inner world of constructive thinking. This transformation all begins with your thoughts. Change your thinking, and you will, you must, change your life. Your job is to create the mental equivalent of what you want to experience in your reality.

Now take some time to think, in light of these mental laws, about how your habitual modes of thought have created every aspect of your life today.

1. Think about your relationships. What in your attitudes, beliefs, expectations, and behaviors is causing your problems with other people?

2. Think about your health. What are your ideas and beliefs about your weight, your level of fitness, your personal appearance, your diet, and your rest?

3. Think about your career. How do your thoughts affect your position, your progress, the quality of your work, and the amount of satisfaction you get from what you do?

4. Think about your level of financial achievement. What would you like to increase or improve? What are your beliefs and expectations concerning your aspirations? How much would you like to earn, and why? And what are your beliefs about that?

5. Think about your inner life, your thoughts, your feelings, your peace of mind and happiness. What beliefs, attitudes, and expectations are creating your world as it is today? Which of them do you want to change?

If you're honest with yourself, you will find that you have self-limiting ways of thinking in one or more of these areas. This is quite normal. Honestly facing the facts about yourself is the starting point of rapid self-improvement.

The Powerhouse of Your Subconscious

Your subconscious mind is an amazing powerhouse that, when properly used, can move you rapidly toward the achievement of your goals and your desires. Your subconscious can be used for creation or destruction, for good or for ill. It can and will make you a prince or a pauper, depending on the way it's programmed.

To fulfill your potential, you must learn how to tap into your subconscious mind at will and use it for your purposes intelligently and constructively.

Once my lawyer was showing me through his offices. He took me into the typing pool, where several secretaries were typing letters and legal documents. Each of the secretaries was hooked into a minicomputer that was available and accessible to all of them. As we left the room, he explained to me that he and his partners had spent more than $100,000 on the computer setup, which they'd purchased about two years before. He told me that when it was first installed, all of the secretaries working there at the time were thoroughly trained on how to use the computer to dramatically increase the quality and quantity of legal work they could produce. Over time, he said, most of the originally trained secretaries had left or gone on to other things. They were replaced one by one with legal secretaries, who unfortunately had no computer training.

"Because we're so busy," he said, "no one has had a chance to go back and train those new secretaries on how to get the most out of our computer system. So now, instead of using this computer for advanced information and word processing, our secretaries simply use it as a glorified typewriter, typing one letter or document at a time, and spending many hours to produce what the minicomputer could produce in a few minutes."

Most people are like those secretaries. They work every day with their minds, but they use this powerful computer for only the most rudimentary tasks. Then they wonder why their work is so hard and why they seem to produce so little. Successful men and women, however, have learned how to operate their conscious and subconscious minds together in harmony, thereby allowing them to achieve their goals far faster and with a great deal less effort.

The Role of the Conscious Mind

Imagine two balls, a golf ball and a basketball, stuck together, with the golf ball on top. This picture represents the relative power and capability of your conscious and your subconscious minds, with the golf ball being your conscious mind and the basketball being your subconscious. Although they have their own separate functions, the two minds are essential to each other.

The conscious mind is the objective or thinking mind. It has no memory, and it can only hold one thought at a time. This mind has four critical functions. Its first function is identification of incoming information received through any of the five senses: sight, hearing, smell, taste, or touch. For example, imagine that you are walking along the sidewalk, and you step out into the street between two cars. At that moment, you hear the roar of an automobile engine. You immediately identify where the sound is coming from and turn and look in the direction of the moving automobile.

The second function of your conscious mind is comparison. The information that you've seen and heard is immediately sent to your subconscious mind for comparison with all of your previous stored information and experiences with moving automobiles. If this car is a block away and moving at thirty miles per hour, using your experience, your subconscious mind will tell you that there's no danger and you can continue walking. If, on the other hand, the car is moving toward you at sixty miles per hour and it's only 100 yards away, you will get a danger message that will require further action on your part.

The third function of your conscious mind is analysis, which always precedes the fourth function: decision making. Your conscious mind functions like a binary computer, accepting or rejecting data and making choices and decisions. It holds only one thought at a time. Positive or negative? Yes or no?

Say you're walking across the street, and you hear the roar of a moving automobile. You see that it's bearing down on you, and your analysis tells you that a decision is required.

The first question is, do I get out of the way? Yes or no? If the answer is yes, then the next question is, do I jump forward, yes or no? If the answer is no, because of cross traffic, then the next question is, do I jump backward? Yes or no?

If the answer is yes, the message is instantaneously transmitted to your subconscious control system. In a split second, your whole body jumps back out of the way. You didn't have to use your conscious mind to think about whether you should put your right foot or your left foot back first. Once your conscious mind gave the command to your subconscious, all the necessary nerves and muscles in your body were coordinated and put into action in a single instant to obey your conscious command.

The Function of the Subconscious

One scholar estimated that the subconscious mind functions at 30,000 times the speed of the conscious mind. You can demonstrate this difference by holding your hand out in front of you and wiggling your fingers. You'll find it's quite easy, because your subconscious mind is controlling the action. Then try to thread a needle and see how much mental effort and concentration are necessary to perform a couple of small movements of your hand, just using your conscious mind.

Your subconscious mind is like a data storage or a memory bank. Its function is to store and retrieve data and keep all of your words and actions consistent with your self-concept and your current mental programming.

Nevertheless, the subconscious mind is subjective: it doesn't think or reason independently; it merely obeys the commands it receives from the conscious mind. If the conscious mind can be thought of as the gardener planting seeds, the subconscious mind can be viewed as the fertile soil in which the seeds sprout and grow. Your conscious mind commands, and your subconscious mind obeys. The subconscious is an obedient servant that works day and night to make your external actions and results fit a pattern consistent with your emotionalized thoughts, hopes, desires, and goals.

Your subconscious will grow either flowers or weeds, whichever you plant by your habitual modes of thinking. The subconscious mind has a homeostatic impulse. It keeps your body temperature at 98.6 degrees Fahrenheit, just as it keeps you breathing and maintains your heartbeat at a certain rate. It maintains a balance among the hundreds of chemicals in your billions of cells so that your entire physical machine for the most part functions in complete harmony. Your subconscious mind also practices mental homeostasis by keeping you thinking and acting in a manner consistent with what you've done and said in the past. All your habit patterns of thinking and acting are stored and maintained in your subconscious mind.

Consequently, your subconscious mind has memorized all your comfort zones, and it works to keep you in them. In the absence of any other instructions from your conscious mind, your subconscious, like a gyroscope or homing beam, will cause you to feel emotionally and physically uncomfortable whenever you move away from your established patterns of thought and behavior. Even if you're moving in the direction of your desired goals, your subconscious keeps you on the track based on the data and instructions that you have previously programmed into it.

The Law of Subconscious Activity

Several laws determine the activity of your subconscious mind. The first is *the law of subconscious activity.* This says that any idea or goal accepted as true by your conscious mind will be accepted as a command by your subconscious mind, which will immediately go to work to bring it into your reality. Your subconscious mind is the seat of the law of attraction, the sending station of mental vibrations and thought energy. When you begin to believe that something is possible for you, your subconscious mind begins broadcasting, and you begin to attract people, circumstances, and opportunities and ideas that are in harmony with your new dominant thoughts and goals.

Any goal accepted as true by your conscious mind will be accepted as a command by your subconscious mind.

The subconscious mind also activates your reticular cortex, often called the reticular activating system. This small finger-like part of the brain regulates the information that you see, hear, and recognize in your environment.

Let's say you decide to buy a red sports car. You'll suddenly start to see red sports cars everywhere. If you start to plan a foreign trip, you'll begin to see articles, information, and posters on foreign places everywhere you go. Your subconscious mind is working to bring to your attention information that you may need to make your thought or goal a reality.

The Law of Concentration

Another important mental law is the *law of concentration*. This law says that whatever you dwell upon grows. The more you think about something, the more it becomes a part of your reality.

The law of concentration is central to all great success. It's used by all high-achieving men and women. When you dwell upon anything, positive or negative, you are commanding your subconscious mind to assign more and more of the capacity of your mental computer toward bringing it into your life. This is why successful people think and talk only about what they want, and unsuccessful people tend to think and talk exactly about the things they don't want. In any case, whatever you dwell upon will begin to grow and become part of your life.

The Law of Substitution

The *law of substitution* is one of the most important of all mental laws. It simply says that you can substitute one thought for another. It's well known that the conscious mind can only hold one thought at a time, positive or negative, but the conscious mind is never empty. It's always thinking about something. Using the law of substitution, you can eliminate any negative, fearful, or anxious thought from your conscious mind by substituting a positive thought in its place.

This powerful method of mental control enables you to keep your mind calm and at peace by choosing to think about something positive (like your goals). Whenever you're faced with a situation that would normally make you upset or angry, a simple way to use the law of substitution is to stop talking and thinking about the problem and to start talking and thinking about the solution. Thinking about a solution is inherently positive, and it will instantly cause your mind to become calm and clear. You can also use the law of substitution by focusing your thoughts on someone you care about or some pleasant idea, like the thought of your next vacation. The main thing is to find ways to keep your mind positive by consciously choosing to replace negative thoughts with positive thoughts.

The Law of Habit

The greatest obstacles to developing the kind of personality you desire and increasing the quality and quantity of your results are your comfort zones, a subject that brings us to the *law of habit*. This law says that everything you are and do is the result of habit. It's like the law of inertia in physics, which says that a body in motion tends to remain in motion unless acted upon by an outside force. In mental terms, the law of habit says that in the absence of a firm decision and a determined effort on your part, you will continue doing and thinking the same things indefinitely. You'll work in the same way, you'll relate to other people, and you'll get the same reactions from them as you've done in the past. You'll eat the same food, engage in the same leisure activities, read the same types of books and publications, and associate with the same kinds of people. You will earn roughly the same amount of money. You will do the same amount of exercise, spend the same amount of time on personal and professional development, and live in the same kind of house, in the same kind of neighborhood, and drive the same kind of car.

Everything you are and do is the result of habit.

Both success and failure are largely the result of habit. Changing your habits is one of the hardest things that you'll ever do, but unless you're an angel already, you have certain habits that you need to discard. There are other habits that are essential to develop. Bad habits are easy to form but hard to live with, whereas good habits are hard to form but easy to live with.

Self-mastery, self-control, and self-discipline are essential habits to develop if you're going to make your life into the glorious experience that is possible for you.

The Law of Practice

There is also the *law of practice*, which says that whatever thought or action you repeat over and over again often enough becomes a new habit. You can develop any habit that you consider necessary or desirable. You can become the person you want to be if you will discipline yourself to act in a way that is consistent with your highest ideals long enough and hard enough for them to become new habits of thought and behavior.

The Law of Emotion

To round off your understanding of the laws that determine the activity of your subconscious mind and everything that happens to you, there's the *law of emotion*. The law of emotion says that 100 percent of your decisions are based on emotion. It used to be said that human beings are 90 percent emotional and 10 percent logical. But now we know that we are, in fact, 100 percent emotional. Every decision you make is determined by the dominant emotion that you are experiencing at that time.

The two major clusters of emotion are fear and desire. As I've already stressed, fear is the great enemy of humankind. It's the cause of all our troubles, and it's a primary reason why people lead lives of quiet desperation, failing to find the health, happiness, and prosperity they seek. Yet most of our decisions are made on the basis of fear rather than on desire. The more decisions we make on the basis of fear—fear of failure, rejection, loss, criticism, poverty, ill health—the more likely we are to have those circumstances repeated in our lives.

But there is a solution, and successful, happy people have found it: use the law of substitution to think about only what you desire and keep your mind off of what you fear. Whatever you dwell upon grows. Your biggest challenge is to dwell upon the things that you want more of in your life. Since your conscious mind can only hold one thought at a time, if you spend all your time concentrating on the things you want, you'll find yourself spending little or no time thinking about the things you don't want.

Here's a little story that illustrates this key point. Many years ago, in ancient Greece, a traveler met an old man on the road and asked him how to get to Mount Olympus. The old man, who turned out to be Socrates, replied by saying, "If you really want to get to Mount Olympus, make sure that every step you take is in that direction." The moral of the story is simple. If you want to be successful and happy, if you want to get to your own Mount Olympus, simply make sure that your every thought and every action are taking you in that direction and not somewhere else.

Sir Isaac Newton is ranked among the greatest scientists who ever lived. His breakthroughs in mathematics and physics laid the groundwork for the modern age. In his later years, he was asked how it was that he, one man, had managed to make such significant contributions to science. He answered by saying, "By thinking of nothing else."

In its simplest terms, success begins with exercising your power of choice and taking systematic, purposeful control over the thoughts that you allow yourself to hold in your conscious mind. By rigorously disciplining yourself to think and talk only about what you want, and by refusing to dwell upon the things that you don't want, you will begin your journey toward the stars.

Now let's look at some ways to bring your subconscious powerhouse to bear on creating a wonderful life.

Awakening from the Sleep of Daily Life

Most people, unfortunately, spend their lives in a form of sleep. They go busily about their daily activities, almost totally preoccupied with a continuous stream of disorganized thought.

You've experienced this phenomenon yourself when you've gotten into your car and driven to work, lost in thought, with almost no memory of the trip afterward. Many of our habitual routines take place with a low level of awareness, as if we were in a mental fog. Sometimes this preoccupation is deliberate—we use it to avoid thinking about parts of our life that we would rather not deal with—but usually it's automatic. We've been going through the motions for so long that our thought processes are fuzzy and unfocused. We only wake up temporarily, when we are shocked, surprised, or caught off guard. As soon as we recover our composure, we slip back into the warm, gentle stream of waking consciousness in which our thoughts flow past in a continual collage of feelings and images.

To become all you can be, it is necessary to become more alert, aware, and awake. It's necessary to take more control over your thought processes so that the combined power of these mental laws is moving you in a direction of your own choosing rather than steering you blindly as a result of your operating on autopilot.

A good way to start this process of awakening is by reflecting on parts of your life, past, present, and future. Begin by imagining that somewhere on the other side of the cosmos, before you were born you had evolved over many lifetimes to become a particular type of person, with a particular set of qualities, interests, talents, and abilities. (It doesn't matter what you think about the idea of reincarnation; this is just an exercise whose point will become clear in a moment.)

To continue with this line of thought, imagine that you deliberately chose your parents and the situation you were born into and brought up in. You did this because at your stage of personal growth and evolution, there were specific lessons about yourself, life, and other people that you had to learn and could learn in no other way except by being born into that family at that time. Imagine also that the person you are today—especially your good qualities—has evolved as a result of the difficult experiences you had growing up, especially as a result of the negative qualities demonstrated by one or both of your parents.

Here's a question for you: if you discovered that you had deliberately chosen your parents, resulting in the person you are today, how would this discovery change your attitude toward your parents and your formative experiences? Would you be more positive and accepting toward them? Would you see yourself and your experiences in a different light? Would you become more philosophical and accepting of apparently difficult times of your life?

Now let's imagine that as you turn this thought over in your mind, you start to see possibilities that you had ignored up to now. Instead of unconsciously seeing yourself as a passive agent or a victim caught up in circumstances beyond your control, you begin to see yourself as an active participant in your own evolution.

Now let's take this exercise further. Imagine that you are here on this earth to do something wonderful with your life, to become an exceptional person and make a significant contribution to your world. Imagine that this is all part of a great master plan that has been carefully designed with your best interests in mind, and that every event and circumstance of your life is an indispensable part of a big jigsaw puzzle whose outline you can only see when you stand back and look at your life as though from a higher plane. Assume that your current situation or difficulty is exactly what you need right now to teach you what you need to know before you can continue your upward journey. Try to see that every experience is a positive one if you view it as an opportunity for growth and self-mastery.

Every experience is a positive one if you view it as an opportunity for growth and self-mastery.

Now project backward, and with calmness, clarity, and a positive mental attitude, think about how every previous experience and situation in your life might have been sent to you at exactly the right time to teach you something you needed to learn so that you could move forward toward the goal that awaits you. Imagine that the events of your life could not have been otherwise than they were. As you develop a healthy acceptance of the complex interconnection of events that have brought you to where you are right now, you'll begin to develop the perspective of the philosopher, of the superior intellect. You will superimpose on your experience a sense of coherence, a feeling that your life is part of something greater than yourself and that everything fits together and happens for a reason.

As you think of your life as a series of events and experiences that are conspiring to help you achieve some great goal or make some great contribution to mankind, you will develop a sense of destiny, which is the hallmark of potential greatness.

Activating the Laws

These simple exercises in self-awareness enable you to begin unlocking the powers of your subconscious mind. Here are some simple suggestions for activating the laws of the universe in a positive way for yourself.

You activate the *law of control* by choosing consciously to view yourself as an active, creative influence in your own life. When you take mental control, you place your hands firmly on the steering wheel of your own destiny. From there, you can begin to determine your own future. By becoming aware of the role of your own thoughts in directing the course of events, you free yourself from the law of accident. Things no longer seem to happen in a random and haphazard way.

You activate the *law of cause and effect* when you stand back from your day-to-day life and reflect upon the incredible number of coincidences that have shaped you into the person you are today. You see that nothing happened by accident: everything has happened and is happening right now as the result of immutable law.

Even if you can't see clearly where your life is going at the moment, you trigger the *law of belief* when you accept that your experiences are leading you toward the accomplishment of something important. The more you think about this eventuality as an inevitable fact, the more likely it is to come true for you. Your beliefs do become your realities.

The *law of expectations* kicks in as you confidently expect to gain something worthwhile, if not essential, from everything that happens to you. This attitude of confident self-expectancy makes your life into more of an adventure, with exciting and unpredictable but happy events occurring to move you toward a positive outcome. You become more optimistic and cheerful, as well as calm and unflappable, and your expectations become your own self-fulfilling prophecies.

Your positive, future-oriented thinking throws the switch on the *law of attraction*, and you begin drawing into your life people and circumstances that are in harmony with your dominant thoughts of hope, optimism, and confidence. The more you think of yourself and your life as uniquely blessed and important, the more your experience will reflect this attitude.

As for the *law of correspondence*, when you see yourself as a special person put on this earth with a special purpose, your outer world of relationships, health, work, and material accomplishments begin to reflect your inner attitudes of mind. As you plant these thoughts into your subconscious by continually holding them in your conscious mind, your subconscious begins to make all your words, feelings, and actions—even your body language—fit a pattern consistent with your new self-concept and goals.

You use the *law of substitution* continually, knowing that your major responsibility is to keep negative thoughts of fear, anger, and self-doubt out of your mind by holding thoughts of faith, hope, and love until they're firmly rooted and growing with a life and power of their own.

You work with the *law of emotion* to keep your thoughts on what you desire and off any and all thoughts of fear. You develop your new attitude by constant repetition until it becomes a new habit.

Most of all, you use the *law of concentration* by dwelling continually on thoughts of courage, hope, love, and belief in yourself and in the wonderful future that life has in store for you. You take time each day to sit and soak your mind in positive and uplifting thoughts, knowing and accepting that whatever you dwell upon long enough and hard enough will eventually materialize in your reality. Your job is to be patient, calm, and trusting. You will achieve what you're meant to achieve when you're ready for it, when your mind is thoroughly prepared. Remember, whatever you want, wants you. Whatever you want is moving towards you right now, just as you are moving toward it. Your primary aim must be to get out of your own way.

Incorporating a new, positive, constructive way of looking at your life, with a bigger picture of past, present, and future, requires thoughtfulness. Developing a superior way of thinking, which harmonizes all the mental laws so that your whole life speeds up in an exciting way, requires that you become more alert, aware, and awake. At first, this may be difficult, but the payoff will be a heightened feeling of self-control and self-mastery—a more positive mental attitude and a tremendous sense of empowerment in every part of your life. You will have put yourself onto the high road to maximum performance and personal achievement.

An Action Exercise

Here's another action exercise for you. Take a sheet of paper and make a list of all the things that you want to see in your life. Write down everything you can think of: happiness, health, good friends, travel, prosperity, financial success, popularity, recognition, the respect of others. Let your imagination run freely.

For the next twenty-four hours, think and talk only about the things on your list. See if you can get through one entire day without criticizing, condemning, complaining, or getting angry, upset, or worried about anything. See if you have the strength of character to think about only what you want for one whole day. This exercise will give you a real insight into where you are in your development. It will also show you how far you have to go.

Major Points

- The universe is governed by laws, both physical and mental.
- You feel positive about yourself to the degree to which you feel you are in control of your life.
- Your thoughts are the only thing over which you have complete control.
- You can shape your life by putting your subconscious mind to work.
- For every effect, there is a specific cause; everything happens for a reason.
- You attract into your life people and situations in harmony with your dominant thoughts.
- You can change your life by unlocking the powers of your subconscious mind.

THREE

Strategic Thinking

Strategic thinking is a skill that you can use to move ahead more rapidly toward your goals than you ever believed possible. This incredibly powerful tool is used by organizations all over the world to maximize their potential and realize their possibilities. It can be an equally powerful method to help individuals realize their full potential for success.

Corporations do strategic planning to increase their return on equity, called ROE. It enables the organization to allocate and reallocate its resources so as to ensure the highest possible return on capital invested in the enterprise. Strategic planning for corporations aims at increasing profitability by increasing the amount of output per unit of input. It revolves around identifying opportunities for the future and systematically moving people and resources from areas of lower productivity to areas of higher productivity.

Personal strategic planning is very similar. Only in this case, your aim is to increase your return on *energy* rather than your return on equity. Your personal equity is human rather than financial capital. More than anything else, you have to invest in and allocate your mental, emotional, and physical energy. Strategic thinking enables you to channel and direct your energies to give you the greatest return on the investment of your time. Personal strategic planning and strategic thinking allow you to allocate your time so that you get more joy, satisfaction, and rewards from everything you do.

Success Is Goals

Not long ago, several successful men and women sat around a large table to discuss the reasons for success and failure. They'd been jointly involved in the production of many books and audio programs on success, and they had known many of the most successful people in America. After considerable discussion, they concluded that success is goals, and all else is commentary: the ability to set goals and to make plans for their accomplishment was more important than any other single skill. They agreed that the ability to think strategically about one's life was the critical skill for high achievement and satisfaction.

Napoleon Hill, author of *Think and Grow Rich*, wrote that anything the mind of man can conceive and believe, it can achieve. Of course, this doesn't mean that you can leap buildings in a single bound, but it does mean that there are virtually no limitations on you when you know exactly what you want to accomplish, write it down, and make a plan for its achievement. This truism is generally recognized by most people, even though very few apply it to their lives.

Anything the mind of man can conceive and believe, it can achieve.

Some time ago I wrote an article for the *National Employment Weekly*. They took one sentence out of the text and blew it up into big letters. It said, "Those who do not have goals are doomed forever to work for those who do." You can either work to achieve your own goals or you can work to achieve the goals of someone else. Ideally, when you work for another company, accomplishing your company's goals should lead to the accomplishment of your own, but in any case, it's always the same. There may be exceptions to this principle, but you can't count on them.

Strategic thinking is the methodology for bringing your mental powers to bear on every area of your life to ensure that you operate with maximum efficiency and effectiveness toward the accomplishment of your goals. Strategic thinking is a rare quality, possessed by less than 1 percent of the population, but in my experience, it can be more helpful than almost any other thinking skill that you can develop.

Start with Values

Strategic thinking begins with standing back and taking a long look at your life. You think about where you are now and where you want to be in the future. Since everything in life is from the inside out, you begin your process of strategic thinking as corporations do: by thinking about and clarifying your values. Values clarification is one of the most important of all exercises. When you decide upon your values—which are the principles that you absolutely believe in and will not compromise—you lay the foundations for a life strategy that enables you to move ahead more rapidly.

Successful people are very clear about what they value, believe in, stand for, and especially what they will *not* stand for. Unsuccessful people, on the other hand, are very fuzzy about their values and often have no values at all. If they've given any thought to their values, they're ready to compromise on them at any time for short-term gain.

Your job is to decide very clearly what your values are and resolve that you will live by them under any circumstances. As you do this, your self-confidence increases, your personality improves, and your results multiply in almost anything you do.

Your job is to decide what your values are and resolve that you will live by them under any circumstances.

True values are engraved in stone. They are inviolable. You either have a value or you don't. You cannot have a value partially, just as you can't be a little bit pregnant. You can't have a value some of the time and not at other times. You cannot have situational values or expedient values, determined by the demands of the current situation. If there's any area of your life where you must be steadfast and true, where you are to be the best person you can possibly be, it is with your values. For example, if you say that integrity is one of your values, you are saying that you will never do anything that is not perfectly upright and honest in each and every area of your life. You will always tell the truth. You will always be honest in all your dealings with other people. You will undergo pain, sacrifice, and financial loss if necessary, but you will not compromise your integrity. One compromise of integrity tears it apart completely. If you compromise your integrity, it is no longer of value and merely becomes a convenient principle to be used for personal advantage whenever it seems to make sense.

The only way that you demonstrate what your values really are is through your actions. It's not what you say, what you intend, or what you wish or hope, but only what you do that reveals what you truly believe and consider important. In fact, you can determine what your values have been in the past by looking back at your previous actions and thinking about how you behaved when push came to shove, when you were under stress and you were forced to choose between alternatives. Every decision you make, every action you take, everything you do represents a choice between what you consider to be more important and what you consider to be less important: between what you value more and what you value less.

When forced, the superior person always chooses the higher value over the lower value. For example, whenever you're confronted with a decision that involves money, you can clear your mind by temporarily putting the thought of money aside and making the right choice: the choice that is consistent with your values. Say to yourself, "It's only money." Leave the money aside and ask, "What is the right and fair thing to do in this situation if no money were involved?" Once you've made the decision based on your values and what's right rather than on finances, you can bring finances back into the equation, and the quality of your decision will be far better for all concerned.

You can choose new values to live by at any time, and you can commit to making them fixed parts of your life. By practicing them on every occasion, you'll eventually internalize them and make them part of your thinking and acting, like breathing in and breathing out. You can make yourself into an extraordinary human being by setting high values and disciplining yourself to live by them on every occasion.

Whom Do You Most Admire?

There are some excellent questions that you can ask to help you determine what your values are and what they should be. A good place to start is to ask yourself, "What three people, living or dead, do I admire the most?" Who are the people whose lives, examples, and teachings have had the greatest influence on your thinking and your beliefs on what is right or wrong, on what is good or bad, what is admirable or unacceptable?

When you think of these three people or anyone else that you look up to, ask yourself, "Why do I admire these people? What values or qualities do they seem to have that I consider to be important and worthy of emulating?"

As I said before, there are three parts to your personality or self-concept. First, there is your *self-ideal*: the person that you most admire and want to be like. Second, there is your *self-image*: the way you see and think about yourself, which guides your performance and controls your behavior. Third, and perhaps the most important, is your *self-esteem*: the way you feel about yourself, how valuable and worthwhile you feel as a human being. Your self-ideal is the person you would like to be in the future, and your self-image is the person you see yourself as being in the present.

Your self-esteem, how much you like and respect yourself, is largely determined by how much you feel that your current behaviors are consistent with the very best person you could possibly be. When you act consistently with your ideals, your self-image improves, and your self-esteem goes up. You like yourself better, and you perform better at everything you do. If you behave in a way that is inconsistent with your ideals, your self-image suffers and your self-esteem goes down, you don't like yourself as much. One of your main jobs in life is to strive to behave more consistently with the very best person you can possibly be. When you do this, you feel happier, more positive, more enthusiastic about yourself, your relationships, and everything you do.

**Your self-esteem is determined by how much
your current behaviors are consistent with
the best person you could possibly be.**

Your self-ideal is the internal mechanism that guides your conscience and your behavior. It's made up of the totality of all the qualities and values of other people that you've admired over the course of your life. For most people, this is probably an unconscious process. You begin to improve yourself when you bring this unconscious process to a more conscious level of awareness and do some serious thinking about it.

Here's an exercise for you: Write down the qualities that you admire most in other people. Think of your parents, your teachers, your coaches, the men and women you've read about over the years, and the ones you look up to when you hear or read about them. Do you admire courage, integrity, determination, honesty, love, compassion, patience, a sense of humor, forgiveness, and persistence? What are the virtues, values, and qualities that you admire most in other people?

Almost invariably, you will find that what you respect the most in others indicates what you most aspire towards yourself. If you admire the courage and integrity of another, it means that you want to develop the qualities of courage and integrity as part of your own character as well. If you admire energy, dynamism, success, and achievement in other people, it means that you want to embody those characteristics in your own personality. The more you admire and respect a certain quality in others, the more likely you are to walk, talk, act, and think like them. You will become what you think about most of the time.

You can live a great life, but you have to make it a great life. It doesn't happen all by itself, and the hardest part of living a great life is to define what that means to you: to define the values and qualities you wish to live by and by which you wish to be known by others. A great life begins when you write your values and ideals down on paper and think about how you can live consistently with them every single day.

Once you've written out your values, organize them in order of priority. Write down your number one value, the value that will take precedence over all others in determining your choices and behaviors. If you have to choose between living consistently with your number one value and any other, you will always choose number one.

When I've done strategic planning for corporations, in every single case the executives selected integrity as their number one value. They recognize that integrity guarantees that you'll live in a manner that is consistent with all the other values. Integrity cannot be compromised without severe penalties. Once you commit yourself to integrity, you are much more likely to adhere to every other value that you write down, even under pressure.

You then write down your second value: the value that takes precedence over all the others except the first. Continue doing this until you've written down your five or six basic values. Although you may have a hundred different values, you need just five or six as your core values. These become the qualities around which you build your life.

Once you've achieved clarity regarding your values, you can organize all of your goals, objectives, and activities in such a way that they are consistent with your values and become extensions of them. You make sure that your inner life and your fundamental beliefs are consistent with your outer life, goals, and activities. Your inner and outer lives should fit together like a hand in a glove.

Your inner and outer lives should fit together like a hand in a glove.

Higher-order values take precedence over lower-order values. Your number one value takes precedence over your number two value. Your number two value takes precedence over your number three value, and so on.

In fact, your order of values can be even more important than the values themselves. For example, imagine that two people both have the same top three values: family, health, and career success. Person A has organized his values so that his number one value is family, his number two value is health, and his number three value is career success. Person B has the same three values but has organized them so that her number one value is career success, her number two value is family, and her number three value is health.

Would there be a difference between person A and person B? Would there be a small difference or a large difference? Would you be able to tell which of these two people you were talking to after you had spoken to them for a couple of minutes? Of course. There would be an extraordinary difference between the two people. It would be immediately obvious and would cause them to be two totally different personalities, even though they had the same values, because of the order in which they have placed those values. Person A would always choose family and the needs of the most important people in his life over health and career success. Person B would always choose career success over family and health. It is only your actions, it is only what you do, that truly indicates your real values both to yourself and to others. You must give a lot of thought to the order of your values and discipline yourself to stick to them no matter what.

Negative Values

Once you've decided on your basic positive values, it's very important to determine your negative values as well. Positive values such as love, health, family, and integrity are pretty easy to identify, but negative values are much subtler and therefore much more dangerous. Just as you are motivated to make choices because of your positive values, you're also motivated to make choices because of your negative values. Each of us has negative values that can be so powerful that they can overwhelm positive ones.

Negative values can easily override positive ones.

Say that you've decided that integrity is your highest value. It can be compromised by the negative value of fear of confrontation. Many people accept treatment from people that makes them feel negative and angry rather than confronting the others and insisting that the treatment be stopped. They are in effect compromising their emotional integrity, which is a positive value, because the fear of confrontation, a negative value, is much stronger in determining their behavior.

The fear of poverty can be a negative value that interferes with and takes precedence over the value of integrity. A person who becomes desperate for money will often do things that are inconsistent with any definition of integrity because the fear of not having enough money is stronger than the desire to live in a way that is consistent with honesty and truth.

Many people have the positive value of success and achievement. This is a good healthy value, and it motivates them to attain higher levels of accomplishment. However, it's very common for this positive value to be negated by the fear of failure. If the fear of failure is greater than the desire for success, the person will be thinking primarily about the possibility of loss rather than the opportunity to gain. This negative value explains why most people in America fail. It's not because they lack the ability, but because their fear of failure overrides their desire for success.

You need to give serious thought to your values. If you're not living consistently with your positive values every day, you need to think honestly about what negative values might be interfering with them. The very act of identifying your negative values (which everyone has) is the first step to eliminating them.

Your Mission Statement

Once you've determined your values, you can move on to the very important job of writing out your mission statement. This is a description of the kind of person you want to be and the kind of life you want to live based on your positive values.

For example, a company may have determined that its values are integrity, quality, service, profitability, and caring about people. The company would write out a mission statement incorporating those values, saying something like this: "We adhere to the highest standards of integrity in producing high-quality products, which we service in an excellent fashion, and earn good profits while respecting the needs of the individuals we work with, inside and outside of the company." This mission statement states what the company stands for, where it is going, and how it is to be judged in terms of success or failure.

The key to your mission statement is to write it in the present tense, as though it were already an objective statement of reality. Project yourself forward and imagine that this mission statement will be perfectly true in every respect five to ten years in the future. It fits the description of the very best person that you could possibly be. It is purely qualitative, based on the values and principles by which you live. It describes the way you honestly wish to be known to others at some future time.

By writing out this mission statement (which few people ever do), you program it deep into your subconscious mind, and you begin to become the person that is consistent with your mission statement. In effect, you are programming these instructions into your sub-conscious computer; you are programming your internal guidance mechanism and organizing your self-ideal so that you'll be inter-nally driven (often unconsciously) to talk and act in a way that is consistent with the standards that you've set for yourself.

The Outer Game of Success

Once you've determined your values and written your mission state-ment, which we call the *inner game of success*, the next step in strategic thinking is to decide what you want to do with your life on the out-side. This is the *outer game of success*, which follows naturally from establishing your values and your mission.

When you have plenty of time, take a pad of paper, sit down by yourself, and write out your dream list. You create your dream list by imagining that you have no limitations whatsoever on what you can do, have, or be. Peak performers in every field engage in this exercise regularly; it's called *blue sky thinking*. You imagine that you have nothing above or around you but a great big blue sky and that you can go in any direction and do anything you want. You let your mind run freely, like a rapidly flowing river, and you think of everything you could ever want to accomplish, as though everything and anything were possible for you.

Imagine that you have no limitations of time or money, no limitations of intelligence, education, or opportunity. Imagine that you have no limitations to assistance or resources. Imagine that everything you need will be available to you if only you can specify on paper exactly what you want. If you're married, do this exercise with your spouse.

Once you've written down everything you can think of, go to phase two: go over the list and divide it into six major categories: *physical, mental, emotional, spiritual, financial,* and *social.* By having goals in each of these areas, you create balance in your life.

Your physical goals are the things that you wish to do with your body. They include not only health and longevity but the activities you'd like to engage in, like climbing a mountain, sailing a boat, skydiving, playing golf, or excelling at tennis. Write down every single physical activity or aspect of your physical life that you think you'd enjoy and that would enhance your life. Don't worry about how possible any of these activities is for the moment. You can evaluate and set priorities for them later.

With regard to your mental or intellectual goals, make a list of all the things you'd like to learn and understand. What languages would you like to learn? What subjects would you like to study? Where would you like to go, and what would you like to participate in that could enrich you and give you a higher quality of mental life? What skills do you need to develop? You may decide that you wish to take additional college courses, read more books, listen to more audio programs, or become knowledgeable about a particular field of endeavor. Just write everything down, without limitations.

Your emotional goals refer to the quality of the relationships that you want to have with the most important people in your life. Describe the quality of the relationship you wish to have with your spouse or mate. What kind of relationship would you like to have with your children? How would you like to get along with your friends and coworkers? How would you like to feel about yourself on an ongoing basis? Would you like to enjoy high levels of self-esteem and self-respect? Set these as goals, and later you'll make plans to ensure that you accomplish them in the shortest period of time.

Your spiritual goals have to do not only with your religious beliefs but with the quality of your inner life. The highest level of spiritual development is to reach a feeling of oneness and peace with the universe, however you choose to call it. Peace of mind and inner contentment have been the motivating influence behind the lives and teachings of all the great mystics and religious thinkers throughout the ages. What are your spiritual goals? What are your goals for inner development and the evolution of your consciousness to higher levels of understanding and inner peace?

Financial and career goals are essential to the accomplishment of everything else. Your ability to earn the money you need will enable you to get most of the other things that you want. You're probably capable right now of earning far more than you're presently earning. The starting point of increasing your income is to sit down with a pad of paper, write out how much you want to earn, and make a plan for its accomplishment. With regard to financial and career goals, you should look around and ask yourself, who else is earning the kind of money I desire? What is he or she doing differently from me?

When you begin achieving success in your career, you will be naturally drawn toward giving something back, toward making a contribution that uplifts the lives of others. Social goals are your goals for contributing to your society and community. Superior men and women are aware that they have a greater obligation to the common good.

Once you have all your goals written out (and sometimes you'll end up with a hundred or more), you begin to sort them out and to organize them by priority.

The ABC Method

The simplest way of prioritizing your goals is the *ABC method*. As you go down your list of goals, you write an A next to every goal that's really important and exciting to you. You write a B next to every goal that you would like to accomplish but which is not as important as your A goals. You then write a C next to every goal that is not as important to you as A and B goals.

Then take all of your A goals under each category and transfer them to a clean sheet of paper. For instance, at the top of one sheet of paper, you would write "financial and career goals." Then you would make a list of all the A financial and career goals that you've identified from your master list. You then set priorities on each of these goals by writing A-1 next to the most important, A-2 next to the second most important, A-3 next to the third most important, and so on. Do this with each of your other goal categories until you have your six areas of life clearly identified with all of your A goals organized in order of priority.

Once you've done this, you will have begun to move toward peak performance. You will have completed an exercise that more than 99 percent of people never complete in their entire lives. You will have begun programming your subconscious mind and activating the law of attraction. Remarkable things will begin to happen to you at a very rapid rate.

Many of my seminar graduates have said that after completing this exercise, their life began to move forward so fast that it was scary. This will happen to you in a very short period of time if you have the discipline to engage in strategic thinking and planning to perform this exercise as I have described. I'll go into this process of goal setting an even greater depth in the next chapter.

When setting goals for any area of your life, one of the most important questions you can ask yourself is, "What are my unique strengths?" What do you do easily and well that seems to be difficult for other people? Looking back over the jobs, careers, and activities that you've engaged in, what things have you accomplished with the greatest pleasure and confidence? What skills, talents, and abilities have accounted for most of your success to date? It's been said that luck is when preparedness meets opportunity. We can also say that success occurs when goals meet natural talents and abilities. You'll be successful to the degree to which you can identify what you do better than anyone else and set goals for accomplishments in that area.

Success occurs when goals meet natural talents and abilities.

There are two aspects of success: being and doing. You know that before you can *do* something, you must first *be* something. You must ask continually, "What kind of a person do I have to become to deserve the kind of success that I desire?" Because of the law of sowing and reaping, you get not what you want in life, but what you deserve. You get only what you have paid for in full in terms of the person that you have become and the things you have done. Thinking about the kind of person you need to be to gain and keep the kind of success that you desire is an important part of strategic thinking.

This is why I've placed so much emphasis on values, both on selecting them and on organizing them by priority. Strategic thinking is thinking about what you're going to have to do minute by minute to live in a way that is consistent with the highest values and principles that you aspire to. This, more than anything else, will determine whether you achieve your internal and external goals.

Two Helpful Questions

Here are two questions that have been very helpful to me in strategic thinking. You should ask them of yourself continually: "What am I trying to do?" and, "How am I trying to do it?"

When you make plans for your life in any of the six areas, you'll find that your plans have defects, which will show up when your plans fail to work as you had expected. This is normal and natural. When this happens, go back to the drawing board and rework your plans. Continue rewriting them until you finally have plans that work the way you want them to. You ask, "What am I trying to do, and how am I trying to do it?"

Many people make the mistake of designing a plan based on the best information they have and then trying to make that plan work without being flexible enough to change it when they run into obstacles. I'm not saying that you should quit when you run into difficulties; I'm saying that you should be able to change the plans when your experience shows that things are not working out as you had expected.

Strategic thinking requires that you always be thinking in terms of how to deploy yourself as a resource more effectively. You keep your vision on the person you want to become and on the goals you want to achieve. You keep writing and rewriting plans and blueprints until they're flawless. You keep your inner life consistent with the person that you want to be, and you keep your outer life activities consistent with the things you want to achieve. Your ability to think strategically is the first part of the master skill of success. Next to it all else is commentary.

Applying Strategic Thinking

The ability to set goals and make plans for their accomplishment is the master skill of success. Developing these skills to the highest possible degree will do more to ensure your success than anything else you could ever learn. Intense goal orientation is an essential characteristic of all high-achieving men and women in every field. You won't realize even a fraction of your potential until you have learned how to set and achieve goals as normally and naturally as you brush your teeth or comb your hair in the morning. Goals are the fuel in the furnace of achievement. A person without goals is like a ship without a rudder, drifting aimlessly and always in danger of ending up on the rocks. A person with goals is like a ship with a rudder, a map, a compass, and a destination, sailing straight and true toward a port of his or her own choosing.

The British historian Thomas Carlyle wrote that a man with a half volition goes back and forth and makes no progress on even the smoothest road, whereas the person with a full volition moves ahead steadily, no matter how difficult the path. Human beings are goal-centered organisms. You are engineered mentally to move progressively and successively from one goal to the other, and you're never really happy unless and until you are moving toward the accomplishment of a worthy objective. Your brain has within it a cybernetic, goal-seeking mechanism that guides and directs you unknowingly over time toward the accomplishment of your goals. In reality, much of goal achieving seems to take place as the result of a natural process. It's the goal setting in the first place that seems to be the most difficult.

It's a truism that each of us is achieving the goals we have set. You are where you are and what you are because you have decided to be there. Your thoughts, your actions, and your behaviors have gotten you to your present position in life, and they could have brought you to no other place. If your goal is to get through the day and go home to watch television, you will probably achieve that goal. If your goal is to be fit and healthy and live a long life, then you'll achieve that too. If your goal is truly to be financially independent or wealthy, there is nothing that can stop you from reaching it sooner or later. Your only limitation is how badly you want it.

Built into your brain are both a success mechanism and a failure mechanism. Your failure mechanism is the natural tendency toward the path of least resistance, the impulse toward immediate gratification, with little or no concern for the long-term consequences of your actions. Your failure mechanism operates automatically, twenty-four hours per day. Every minute, every hour, it ticks away, and most people allow their desire for what is fun and easy and convenient to determine all of their decisions and actions.

However, you also have a success mechanism built into your brain. It overrides your failure mechanism, and it is triggered by a goal. The bigger your goal and the more intensely you desire it, the more likely you will be to exert your powers of self-discipline and willpower to make you do the things that you need to do to achieve your goal.

Setting goals and planning for their accomplishment is the master skill of success.

After a career of fifty years, during which he worked with and trained more than 20,000 salespeople, Elmer Letterman concluded that the one quality that would most predict success was what he called "intensity of purpose." Taking any two people with the same relative levels of intelligence, background, education, and experience, the one with the greatest intensity of purpose would always be the most successful.

The famous oil billionaire H. L. Hunt went bankrupt raising cotton in Arkansas as a young man. He then moved to Texas, won an oil lease in a poker game, and went on to build a fortune of several billion dollars and become one of the world's richest men. He was once asked his formula for success. He said that in America, you only needed two things to be successful. First, he said, decide exactly what it is you want. Most people never do that. Second, determine the price you're going to have to pay to get it, and then resolve to pay that price.

We only know two things for sure about the price of success. First, in order to get the success you desire, however you define it, you must pay the price in full. You must sow before you reap, and you may have to work a long time before you harvest the crop. Second, you have to pay the full price in advance. Success is not like sitting down in a restaurant where you can pay the bill after you've enjoyed the dinner. The success that you desire requires payment in full, in advance, every single time. And how can you tell if you've paid the full price of success? That's easy. When you've paid the full price, the success will be there in front of you for all to see, by law, not by chance. When you've sown, you will reap—cause and effect, action and reaction.

Applying the Mental Laws

I've already discussed several mental laws. Sometimes people are unsure about how they're going to remember to use and apply all of them. It's easy when you have a clearly defined goal toward which you're working every day; all the laws work automatically and in harmony with your purposes.

The greatest enemy of success, as I've said, is the comfort zone, the tendency to get stuck in a rut and resist all change, even positive change, that would force you out of your comfort zone. We naturally tend to fear and avoid change. We want things to stay the same, but to get better too. However, all growth, progress, and advancement require change, and in spite of anything that we do, life never goes on the same way for very long; it's always changing in one direction or another. Things are either improving or deteriorating, but they never stay the same.

The law of control says that you feel positive about yourself to the degree to which you feel you're in control of your own life. Goal setting enables you to control the direction of change in your life and thereby assure that that change is predominantly positive and self-determined. No one fears a change that represents an improvement. With clear goals, backed by detailed plans of accomplishment, you take full control over your life and move boldly forward in the direction of positive change.

The law of cause and effect says that for every effect in your life, there's a specific cause. Goals are a cause; achievement is an effect. You sow goals and you reap results. Goals begin as thoughts or causes and manifest themselves as conditions or effects.

You trigger the law of belief by intensely believing that you will achieve your goals and by taking actions consistent with those beliefs. Your beliefs or goals eventually become your reality.

You trigger the law of expectations by constantly expecting that everything that is happening, positive or negative, is moving you toward the realization of your goals. You look for something positive or beneficial in every event, and you soon get what you expect.

You activate the law of attraction by thinking continually about your goals. With your goals as your dominant thoughts, you invariably begin to attract into your life people and circumstances that are in harmony with achieving those goals.

The law of correspondence says that your outer world will correspond with your inner world. When your inner world is dominated by thoughts and plans of how to achieve the things that are important to you, your outer world of manifestation and effect will soon mirror your inner world of goals and plans.

The law of subconscious activity says that whatever thoughts you hold in your conscious mind, your subconscious mind goes to work to bring into your reality. When you think about your goals, more and more of your subconscious computing capability is allocated toward making your words and actions fit a pattern consistent with what you want to achieve.

The law of concentration says that whatever you dwell upon grows. What do you dwell upon continually? Your goals.

The law of substitution says that you can substitute a positive thought for a negative one. What positive thought do you use to substitute for negative thoughts or experiences? Your goals. Whenever something goes wrong, think about your goals. Whenever you have a bad day, think about your goals. The very thought of something that you want to accomplish in the future is inherently positive and uplifting. It's impossible to think about your goals continually and be anything else but optimistic and highly motivated.

The law of habit says that almost everything we do is the result of our habits, either good or bad. What new habits do you want to form? You want to form the habit of regularly and systematically setting, resetting, and reviewing your goals every single day.

The law of practice says that whatever you practice over and over again becomes a new habit. By using the law of practice, you'll soon develop the lifelong habit of perpetual goal setting and goal achieving.

Whatever you practice over and over again becomes a new habit.

When you begin using these mental laws for a clearly defined purpose to which you're totally committed, you become an unstoppable powerhouse of mental and physical energy. With clear, specific goals, you can develop and use all of your mental powers and accomplish more in the next few years than most people accomplish in a whole lifetime.

Major Points

- Strategic thinking begins with establishing your values.
- What you most admire in others reflects what you most aspire to.
- Once you have established your values, begin to organize your goals.
- Write out a mission statement: a description of who you want to be based on your positive values.
- Create a dream list by imagining that you have no limitations on what you can do, have, or be.
- Setting goals is the master skill of success.
- You must sow before you reap.

FOUR

The Benefits of Goal Setting

With everything that we know about strategic thinking and goal setting, you might think that everybody would be doing it. You've probably been told for years that you have to have goals and you have to be working towards them on a regular basis. Yet the sad fact is that very few people have goals at all. Less than 3 percent of the population have written goals. Fewer than 1 percent of the population read and review their goals on a regular basis. Many people have attended seminars, read books, and listened to audio recordings on goal setting, yet if you ask them if they have clear written goals and plans for their accomplishment, they will confess sheepishly that they don't. They know they're supposed to have goals and they intend to set some goals fairly soon, but they just haven't gotten around to it yet.

Why People Don't Set Goals

When I began studying and applying these principles of success, I got such extraordinary results that I eagerly shared this information with anyone who would listen. That's how I began speaking in public and doing seminars. However, I was constantly amazed at how enthusiastically people would agree with me and then go away and do nothing. So I began to analyze and try to figure out why it was that people don't set goals. I've concluded that there are basically seven reasons. It's important to think about them and determine whether or not they apply to your situation.

The first reason people don't set goals is that they are simply not serious. They're talkers instead of doers. They want to be more successful, they want to improve their lives, but they are not willing to make the necessary efforts. They don't have the burning desire to make something of themselves, to make their lives bigger and better and more exciting. You can only tell what a person really believes by their actions, not their words. It's not what you say or what you intend or what you wish or hope or pray for, but only what you do that counts. Your true values and beliefs are always and only expressed in your actions. One person who will take action is worth ten brilliant talkers who end up doing nothing. I get countless phone calls, letters, and proposals from all kinds of people with all kinds of ideas, but the only ones who impress me are the ones who actually do something. Only action is action, and nothing else counts for much. Don't tell people what you're going to do; show them.

**Your true values and beliefs are always
and only expressed in your actions.**

The second reason that people don't set goals is that they have not yet accepted responsibility for their lives. I used to think that goals were the starting point of success until I realized that until a person accepts that they are fully responsible for their life and everything that happens in it, they will not even take the first step toward goal setting. Irresponsible people are still waiting for real life to begin. They use up all their creative energy making elaborate excuses for their failure to make progress; then they buy lottery tickets and go home and watch television.

The third reason people don't set goals has to do with the terribly destructive effects of guilt. A person who is so low mentally and emotionally that they have to look up to see bottom is not the kind of person who can confidently and optimistically set goals for the next few years. A person who's been raised in a negative environment, leaving him or her with feelings of being undeserving and the attitude of what's the use? is not really capable of goal setting. If you meet a person like this, you should realize that they're very hard to help.

The fourth reason people don't set goals is that they don't realize their importance. If you're raised in a household where your parents don't have goals and where setting and achieving goals is not a regular family discussion topic, you can reach adulthood without even knowing that there are such things as goals outside of sports.

I had personally never even heard of goals or goal setting until I was twenty-three years old and I stumbled across a copy of *Think and Grow Rich* by Napoleon Hill. If you move in a social circle where people don't have clearly defined goals toward which they're working on a regular basis, it'll be easy for you to assume that goals are not particularly important. Since 80 percent of the people around you are going nowhere, if you are not careful, you'll end up drifting with the crowd, following the followers, and going nowhere as well. If people knew that all their hopes and dreams and plans for the future, all their aspirations and ambitions, depend upon their ability and willingness to set goals, if people realized how important goals are to a happy, successful life, I think far more people would have goals than they do today.

The fifth reason people don't set goals is that they don't know how. You can complete an advanced university degree, with sixteen or seventeen years of education, and never receive one hour's worth of instruction on goal setting, even though it is more important than any other single subject that you could ever learn in assuring your long-term happiness.

An even worse mistake is to assume that you already know how to set goals. A person who already assumes that they know a critical skill when their understanding of it is rudimentary is in great danger of failure. I've been studying goal setting and practicing goal setting techniques for decades, I've taught countless men and women how to set goals, and I've done strategic planning and goal setting for billion-dollar corporations. I don't know anyone who has studied and applied these concepts as thoroughly as I have, and still I feel that I have a lot to learn. If a person really has goal setting down cold, he or she is probably either very rich or very happy or both.

The sixth reason people don't set goals is the fear of rejection or criticism. From the time we were children, our dreams, fantasies, and ideas have been slapped down by the criticism and laughter of others. Maybe our parents didn't want us to get our hopes up or be disappointed, so they quickly pointed out all the reasons why we wouldn't be able to achieve our goals. Our siblings and friends might have ridiculed us for thinking about being someone or doing something far beyond what they had accomplished. Children are not dumb. They soon learn that if you want to get along, you go along. Over time, an intelligent child living under these conditions gradually stops coming up with new ideas or goals. It's just not worth the trouble.

Here's the solution to the fear of criticism: keep your goals confidential. All excellent goal setters learn to keep their goals to themselves. Don't tell anybody. No one can laugh at you or criticize you if they don't know what your goals are. The only exceptions are people, such as your boss or your spouse, whose help you'll need to achieve your goals; you should also share your goals with other goal-oriented people.

By the way, a good policy is to encourage everyone who tells you about a goal they have. Tell them to go for it. Tell them they can do it. Encouraging others motivates you too. It's one of the best applications of the law of sowing and reaping. If you would like others to encourage you, take every opportunity to encourage them.

The seventh and most important reason that people don't set goals is the fear of failure. This is the greatest single obstacle to success. It keeps people in their comfort zones, keeping their heads down and playing it safe as the years speed by. The fear of failure is expressed in the attitude of "I can't, I can't, I can't." It's learned in early childhood through criticism and punishment for doing things your parents disapproved of. This fear does more to paralyze hope and kill ambition than any other negative emotion.

Most people fear failure because they don't understand the role of failure in achieving success. The rule is simply this: it's impossible to succeed without failing. Failure is an indispensable prerequisite for success. The greatest failures in human history have also been the greatest successes. In the same year that Babe Ruth was the home run king of baseball, he also struck out more than any other player.

Failure is an indispensable prerequisite for success.

Success is a numbers game. There's a direct relationship between the number of things that you try and your probability of success. Even if you were the worst baseball player in the American League, if you swung with all your heart at every ball that came over the plate, the law of probability says that you must eventually get a hit, and you will finally get a home run. The key is to swing with all your might and keep swinging without worrying about striking out occasionally. Napoleon Hill said, "Within every adversity is the seed of an equal or greater opportunity or advantage."

Success is a numbers game.

The way to deal with temporary failure is to seek within every setback for a valuable lesson. Become an inverse paranoid: convince yourself that everything that's happening to you is moving you toward the achievement of your goal, even when it seems to be moving you away.

Most great successes were preceded by great failures. Decide in advance to take every setback as a spur to greater effort (especially in business and sales), knowing that you're getting closer and closer to success with every experience. Look upon temporary defeat as a signpost that says, "Stop. Go this way or that way instead." One five-year study showed that a key quality of leaders was that they never used words like *failure* or *defeat*. Instead, they used words like *valuable learning experiences* or *temporary glitches*. You can overcome the fear of failure—the major reason people don't succeed—by accepting temporary failure and setbacks as inevitable parts of your ultimate success.

Five Principles of Goal Setting

Strategic thinking and goal setting can be a powerful, even a life-changing experience, and there are five basic principles of goal setting that are essential for high achievement.

Principle number one is the principle of *congruency*: in order to perform at your best, your goals and your values must fit together like a hand in a glove. Your values represent your deepest convictions about what is right and wrong, what is good and bad, and what is important and meaningful to you. You will only achieve high performance and high self-esteem when what you're doing, your goals, and what you believe to be important—your values—are in complete harmony.

The second principle of goal setting is your *area of excellence*. Each person has the capacity to be excellent at something—maybe many things—and you can only achieve your full potential by finding your area of excellence and developing your talents in that area. The inspirational author Emmett Fox called this "your heart's desire." You'll never be happy or satisfied until you find it and commit your life to it. It's the one thing that you are uniquely capable of doing with excellence. Your area of excellence may change as your career evolves, but all truly successful men and women have found their areas of excellence and put their whole hearts into becoming outstanding in those fields.

**You can only achieve your full potential
by finding your area of excellence.**

The third principle of goal setting is the *acres of diamonds concept*. "Acres of Diamonds" was the title of a talk by Russell Conwell, founder of Philadelphia's Temple University, around the turn of the twentieth century. The talk became so popular that he was eventually asked to give it more than 5,000 times, word for word. The essence of the story is that the opportunity you are looking for probably lies right under your own feet, right where you are, right now.

In the story, an old farmer became very excited one day upon hearing of men who had gone off into Africa, discovered diamond mines, and become fabulously wealthy. He decided to sell off his farm, organize a caravan, and head into the vastness of Africa to find diamonds and crown his life with fabulous wealth.

For many years, he searched the vast African continent for diamonds. Eventually he ran out of money, and finally, alone in a fit of despair, he threw himself into the ocean and drowned.

Meanwhile, back on the farm that he had sold, the new farmer was out watering a donkey one day in a stream that cut across the farm. He found a strange stone that threw off light in a remarkable way, and he took it into the house and thought no more of it.

Some months later, a merchant traveling on business stopped for the night at the farm and saw the stone. He grew very excited, and he asked if the old farmer had finally returned. No, the old farmer had never been seen again; why was the merchant so excited? He picked up the stone and said, "This is a diamond of great price and value." The new farmer was skeptical, but the merchant insisted that he show him where he'd found the diamond. They went out on the farm to where the farmer had been watering the donkey. As they looked around, they found another diamond, and another, and then another. It turned out that the whole farm was covered with acres of diamonds. The old farmer had gone off to Africa seeking for diamonds without ever looking under his own feet.

Likewise, your acres of diamonds probably lie under your own feet, although they're probably disguised as hard work. It's been said that opportunities come dressed in work clothes. Your acres of diamonds probably lie in your own talents, your interests, your education, your background and experience, your industry, your city, your contacts. Your acres of diamonds probably lie under your own feet if you will take the time to go to work on them.

The fourth principle for success in goal setting is the principle of *balance*. It says that you need a variety of goals in the six critical areas of life in order to perform at your best. Just as a wheel on an automobile must be balanced to go around smoothly, in order for your life to proceed smoothly, you must have your goals in balance. You need family and personal goals. You need physical and health goals. You need mental and intellectual goals, goals for study and personal development. You need career and work goals. You need financial and material goals. Finally, you need spiritual goals: goals aimed at inner development and higher understanding. To maintain balance, you need two or three goals in each area: a total of twelve to eighteen in all.

This balance will enable you to be working on something important to you all the time. When you're not working on your job, you can be spending time with your family. When you're not developing yourself physically, you can be working on personal and professional development. When you're not engaging in meditation, contemplation, and other inner development work, you can be working on tangible material goals.

The fifth principle of goal setting is your *major definite purpose* or mission statement for your life. Your major definite purpose is your number one goal: the goal that is more important to you than any other single goal or objective at this time. You may have a variety of goals, but you can only have one major definite purpose. The failure to choose an overarching, dominating major goal is the primary reason for diffusion of effort, wasting of time, and the failure to advance.

Your major definite purpose is your number one goal: the goal that is more important to you than any other.

You choose your major definite purpose by analyzing and asking, "Which goal, if I accomplish it, would do the most to help me achieve all my other goals?" Usually this is a financial goal, but sometimes it can be a health or relationship goal instead. The selection of your major definite purpose is the starting point of all great success and achievement. This then becomes your mission, the organizing principle for all your other activities. Your major definite purpose becomes the catalyst that activates the laws of belief, attraction, and correspondence. The person with an exciting major goal starts to make rapid progress in spite of all obstacles and limitations.

Seven Goal Setting Questions

Here are the seven main goal setting questions that you can ask and answer over and over again.

1. What are your five most important values in life right now? This question will help you clarify what is really important to you, and by extension, what is less important or unimportant. Once you've identified the five most important values to you, organize them in order of priority from number one—the most important—through to number five. Because you live from the inner to the outer and your values define your innermost convictions, your choice of values comes before setting goals. Clarity

concerning your values enables you to select goals that are consistent with what's really important to you.

2. What are your three most important goals in life right now? Write the answer to this question within thirty seconds; this is called the *quick list method*. When you only have thirty seconds to write your three most important goals or problems, your subconscious mind sorts them out quickly, and they just pop into your conscious mind. In thirty seconds, your answers will be as accurate as if you had thirty minutes.

3. What would you do, and how would you spend your time if you learned today that you only had six months to live? This is another question to help you clarify what you really care about, and especially *whom* you really care about. Someone once said that you're not ready to live until you know what you would do if you only had one hour left on earth. What would you do? Write it down.

4. What would you do, how would you change your life, if you won $1 million cash, tax-free, tomorrow? What would you do differently? What would you buy? What would you start or stop doing? Imagine that you only have two or three minutes to write the answer and that you'll only be able to do or have what you have written. This question will help you decide what you would do if you had all the time and money you need—if you had no fear of failure.

5. What have you always wanted to do but been afraid to attempt? What have you always wished that you could do, but something has held you back? This question helps you see where your fears could be blocking you from doing what you really want to do.

6. What do you most enjoy doing in the whole world? Put another way, what do you really love to do? Which activities give you

your greatest feelings of self-esteem and satisfaction? This is another values question, and it may indicate where you should explore to find your heart's desire.

7. Perhaps this is the most important question: imagine that a genie appeared with a magic wand and granted you one wish. The genie guarantees that you will be absolutely, completely successful in any one thing that you attempt to do, big or small, short or long-term. What one great thing would you dare to dream if you knew you could not fail? If you were absolutely guaranteed of success in any one thing, big or small, short or long-term, what one exciting goal would you set for yourself?

Whatever answer you write to any of these questions, the very fact that you could write it down means that you can achieve it. Once you've identified what you want, the only question is, "Do I want it badly enough, and am I willing to pay the price?"

Once you've identified what you want, the only question is, "Do I want it badly enough, and am I willing to pay the price?"

An Action Exercise

Now that you know the questions to ask, here is an action exercise for you. Take a few minutes with a pad and write out the answers to each of the questions above. Once you have your answers on paper, go over them and select just one as your major definite purpose in life right now. By doing this, you will move yourself into the top 3 percent: you will have established a written set of goals for yourself. You are now ready to make a plan and move ahead rapidly.

Major Points

- Failure is an important part of success.

- Seek within every setback for a valuable lesson.

- There are five basic principles of goal setting: congruency, finding your area of excellence, the acres of diamonds concept, balance between goals, and a major definite purpose.

- Use the seven goal setting questions to clarify your purpose.

FIVE

The Twelve-Step Process

As we've seen, the most important success habit you can develop is continual goal setting, and the most important action you can take is to set and achieve one clear, challenging goal. When you set a goal and achieve it, you move from the realm of positive thinking into the realm of positive knowing.

Your job is to get yourself to the point where you know beyond the shadow of a doubt that you can set and achieve any goal that you desire. From that point on, your future is unlimited, and you become unstoppable. The thrill of achievement, the feeling of having overcome adversity and winning in spite of the odds, releases endorphins in your brain and gives you pleasure and excitement that can come from no other source.

The habit of continual goal setting, of using all your mental powers, eventually becomes a positive addiction. You'll get to the point where you can hardly wait to get up and start your day, and you'll hate to go to bed at night. You'll become so positive and self-confident that your friends will hardly recognize you.

**The habit of continual goal setting eventually
becomes a positive addiction.**

The most difficult mental obstacle to overcome is inertia: the tendency to slip back into a comfort zone and lose your forward momentum. Perhaps the best definition of character is the ability to carry through on a resolution after the mood in which the resolution was made has passed.

Anyone can set goals, and many people do. Probably half the population makes resolutions every New Year's Eve, but that's not enough. It's the way the goals are set and the way plans are made to accomplish them that determines what happens afterward.

To maximize your goal achieving ability, you need a systematic method. You need a proven process that you can use over and over, with any goal in any situation, to bring all the powers of your mind to bear in accomplishing anything you desire.

The twelve-step process that you're about to learn is perhaps the most powerful ever developed. It has been used by hundreds of thousands of men and women all over the world to revolutionize their lives. It's been used by corporations to reorganize internally so that they can go on to greater success and profitability. It is simple, as all true things are simple, but it is so effective that it continues to amaze even the skeptics.

The whole purpose of this process is to create within your mind the mental equivalent of what you wish to achieve in your external world. The law of mind says that your thoughts objectify themselves. You become and you accomplish what you think about, and if you think about it with tremendous clarity and vividness, it can happen much faster than you can imagine. There's a direct relationship between how clearly you can see your goal as accomplished in your mind and how rapidly it appears in your life. This twelve-step process takes you from fuzziness to clarity and gives you a track to run on to wherever you want to go.

Step One: Desire

Step one in setting and achieving goals is *desire.* This motivational force enables you to overcome the fear and inertia that hold most people back.

As we've seen, probably the greatest obstacle to success is fear. It is the reason for the tendency to sell yourself short and settle for far less than you're capable of. The law of emotion says that you make every decision based on emotion—either of fear or of desire. It also says that a stronger emotion will overcome a weaker emotion. The law of concentration says that whatever you dwell upon grows. If you dwell upon your desires, if you think about them, write them out, and plan around them continually, your desires grow in intensity. They eventually become so strong that they push aside your fears. Your burning desire for achievement enables you to overcome your natural inertia toward the path of least resistance.

You make every decision based on emotion.

Desire is invariably personal. You can only want something for yourself, not because you feel someone else wants it for you. In setting your major definite purpose, you must be perfectly selfish. You must be absolutely clear about what you want to be and have and do. If you could only achieve one great goal in life, what would it be? Why are you on this earth? What is your reason for existence?

What kind of achievement would give you the greatest amount of happiness and satisfaction?

The quality required for great success, and especially for the achievement of wealth, is burning desire, a powerful emotion that overcomes all obstacles in its path, like a flash flood. If you want it badly enough and long enough and hard enough, there's virtually nothing that can stop you from achieving it. Desire is the starting point.

Step Two: Belief

The second step in goal setting is *belief.* In order to activate your subconscious mind and (as you will soon learn) your superconscious capabilities, you must absolutely believe that it is possible for you to achieve your goal. You must have faith that you deserve the goal and that it will come to you on schedule, when you're ready for it. Your faith and belief must deepen into an absolute conviction that the goal is achievable for you. Because belief is the catalyst that activates your mental powers, it's important that your goals be realistic and believable, especially at first.

**You must have faith that you deserve your goal
and that it will come to you on schedule.**

If your goal is to earn more money, set a goal to increase your income by 25 to 50 percent over the next twelve months. That's a goal that you can get your mind around. It's believable and can therefore be a source of motivation. If the goal is too far beyond anything you've accomplished, it becomes a demotivator: you easily become discouraged and soon stop believing that it's possible for you.

Completely unrealistic goals are a form of self-delusion, and you cannot delude yourself into goal attainment. It requires hard, practical, systematic effort, working in harmony with the principles we've been discussing here. If you want to lose weight, don't set a goal to lose thirty, forty, or fifty pounds. Instead, set a goal to lose five pounds over the next thirty to sixty days. When you have lost the first five pounds, set a new goal to lose another five pounds, and so on until you've achieved your ideal weight. A five-pound weight loss is believable, whereas a weight loss of thirty, forty, or fifty pounds is hard to accept as possible.

One of the kindest and most helpful things you can do for your children is to help them to set realistic and achievable goals. They need to develop the habit of setting and achieving goals—although not necessarily the ability to set big goals. There's an old saying that if you save your pennies, the dollars will take care of themselves. If your children develop the habit of setting and achieving small goals, they will eventually move on to medium-size goals and then on to larger ones.

Before you can accomplish big goals, major efforts are necessary. Sometimes you'll require weeks and months and years of hard work and preparation before you'll be ready to achieve big goals. You must pay your dues in advance. Unless you're extraordinarily brilliant or talented, you must be honest with yourself and accept that if the goal is worth achieving, it's worth working for patiently and persistently.

Many people set goals that are far beyond their capacity to achieve. They work at them for a little while, and then they quit. They become discouraged, and they conclude that goal setting doesn't work, at least not for them. This primarily happens because they've tried to do too much too fast.

Your main responsibility with regard to the power of belief is to create and maintain a positive mental attitude by confidently expecting that if you continue to do certain things in a certain way, you will eventually attract the people and the resources necessary to reach your goal right on schedule, right when you're ready for it.

Step Three: Write It Down

Step three in goal setting is to *write it down*. Goals that are not in writing are not goals at all. They're merely wishes or fantasies. A wish has been defined as a goal with no energy behind it—a bullet with no powder in the cartridge. When you write down a goal on a piece of paper, however, you crystallize it; you make it concrete and tangible. You can pick it up and look at, hold, touch, and feel it. You have taken it out of the air and put it into a form that you can do something with.

One of the most powerful methods for programming a goal into your subconscious mind is to write it out clearly, vividly in detail, exactly as you would like to see it in reality. Remember, decide what's right before you decide what's possible. Decide what you really want before you begin to worry about your limitations. Make the description of your goal ideal in every respect; leave no detail out. Don't worry for the moment about how the goal is going to be achieved. In the beginning, your main job is to be absolutely certain about exactly what you desire rather than the process of achieving it.

Some years ago, in the middle of a recession, my wife and I had to sell our home to raise cash and pay our bills. We moved into a rented house temporarily and ended up living there for two years. During this time, we decided to get serious about our dream home. Even though we had little money, we subscribed to several magazines filled with pictures and descriptions of beautiful homes. About once a week, Barbara and I would sit down and page through these magazines, discussing the various features that we would like to see in our ideal home. We put all thought of cost, location, and down payment temporarily out of our minds. We eventually drew up a list of forty-two features that we felt would constitute the perfect home for us and our family. We then put the list away, put our heads down, and continued to work.

Three years passed, and a thousand things happened. After two years, we moved out of the rented house and into a home that we purchased. All kinds of unexpected and unpredictable events took place, and when the dust finally settled, we were in a beautiful 5,000-square-foot home in sunny San Diego, California.

While we were unpacking our belongings, we found the list. The house that we had bought turned out to have forty-one of the forty-two features that we had written down three years before. The only detail it lacked was a built-in vacuum cleaner, which was perhaps the least important. This is just one of a hundred stories that I could tell you about writing down your goals and thinking about them all the time.

The most important reason for writing down your goals, aside from clarifying them in your mind, is that the very act of writing them down intensifies your desire and deepens your belief that they are achievable. The primary reason that people don't write down their goals is that deep in their hearts, they don't think it will do any good. However, when you discipline yourself to write down your goals, you override your failure mechanism, and you turn on your success mechanism to full power.

Writing down your goals overrides your failure mechanism.

Step Four: List the Benefits

Step four in goal achieving is to *make a list of all the ways that you will benefit from achieving your goal.* Just as goals are the fuel in the furnace of achievement, reasons are the force that intensifies your desire and makes you unstoppable. Your motivation depends on your motives—your reasons for acting in the first place—and the more reasons you have, the more motivated you will be.

There's a story about a young man who came to Socrates and asked him how he could gain wisdom. Socrates asked the young man to come with him, and they walked together into a nearby lake. When the water got to be about four feet deep, Socrates suddenly grabbed the young man, pushed his head under the water, and held it there. The young man thought it was a joke at first and didn't resist, but as he was held under the water longer and longer, he became frantic. He struggled desperately to get free as his lungs burned for lack of oxygen. Finally Socrates let him up, coughing and sputtering and gulping for air. Socrates said, "When you desire wisdom with the same intensity that you desire to breathe, nothing will stop you from getting it."

Your job is to keep your desire burning brightly by continually thinking of all the benefits, satisfactions, and pleasures that you will enjoy as a result of achieving your goal. Each person is motivated and excited by different things. Some people are excited by money and the possibility of living in a big house and driving a beautiful car; others are motivated by recognition, status, and prestige—by the idea of earning the respect of others. The famous author E. M. Forster once said, "I write to gain the respect of those I respect."

Make a list of all the benefits, tangible and intangible, that you could possibly enjoy as a result of achieving your goal. You'll find that the longer the list, the more motivated, determined, and unstoppable you will become. If you have one or two reasons for achieving a goal, you'll have a moderate level of motivation, but you'll be easily discouraged when the going gets rough (as it surely will). If you have twenty or thirty or fifty reasons for achieving a goal, you will become like an irresistible force of nature. Nothing will discourage you from keeping on until you accomplish what you've set your mind on.

Step Five: Analyze Your Position

Step number five in goal setting and achieving is to *analyze your position*, your starting point. If you decide to lose weight, the first thing to do is to weigh yourself. If you want to achieve a certain net worth, first create a personal financial statement to find out how much you're worth today. Determining your starting point also gives you a baseline from which you can measure your progress. I cannot emphasize too strongly that the clearer you are about where you're coming from and where you're going, the more likely you will be to end up where you want to be.

Step Six: Set a Deadline

Step six in goal setting is to *set a deadline*. You should set a deadline on all tangible, measurable goals, such as increases in income or net worth, or improvements in your health, such as weight loss or running a certain number of miles. When you set a deadline for a tangible goal, you program it into your mind and activate your subconscious forcing system, which, in most cases, ensures that you accomplish your goal by that date at the latest.

It's better not to set a deadline on intangible goals, like the development of patience, kindness, compassion, or self-discipline. When you set a deadline for the development of a personal quality, this same forcing system ensures that that will be the day you first begin to demonstrate the chosen quality.

Often people resist setting deadlines for fear they will not achieve their goals by the deadline. They do everything possible to avoid feelings of discouragement. What if you do set a deadline and you don't achieve your goal by the deadline? Simple: you set another deadline. It just means that you're not ready yet. You guessed wrong. If you don't achieve your goal by your new deadline, you set still another deadline until you finally do achieve your goal.

**If you don't achieve your goal by your deadline,
set another deadline.**

My friend Don Hudson says there are no unrealistic goals, merely unrealistic deadlines, but probably in 80 percent of cases, if your goal is sufficiently realistic, your plans are sufficiently detailed, and you work them faithfully, you will achieve it on or before your deadline.

If your major definite purpose has a two- or three- or five-year deadline, the next step is to break your goal down into ninety-day subgoals, then break the ninety-day subgoals further down into thirty-day subgoals. With your long-term goal as your organizing principle, you can more readily set realistic short-term and medium-term goals that enable you to keep on track.

Step Seven: List the Obstacles

Step number seven in goal attainment is to *make a list of all the obstacles* that stand between you and the accomplishment of your goal. Great obstacles exist wherever great success is possible. In fact, obstacles are the flip side of success and achievement. If there are no obstacles between you and your goal, it is probably not a goal at all, merely an activity.

When you've listed every single obstacle that you can think of, organize the list in order of importance. What is the biggest single obstacle that stands between you and your goal? I called this your *rock*. On the pathway to the accomplishment of anything worthwhile, there will be a series of obstacles, detours, and roadblocks, but almost invariably there is one big rock or major obstacle that lies across the road and blocks your progress. Focus on removing this rock before you get bogged down in dealing with smaller obstacles and problems.

The obstacle or rock may be internal or external. If it's internal, it may be that you lack a particular skill, ability, or attribute that's essential to achieving your goal. You must be very objective and ask yourself, "Is there anything about myself that I will have to change, or any ability that I will have to develop, in order to achieve my goal?"

The obstacle may be external. You may find that you're in the wrong job, with the wrong company, in the wrong relationship, or even in the wrong industry. You may need to start over, doing something else somewhere else, if your goal is to be achieved.

So what is your rock?

Step Eight: Identify the Information You Need

Step number eight is to *identify the additional information* that you will need in order to achieve your goal. We live in an information-based society, and the most successful people are those who have the information they require.

Almost all mistakes that you make in your financial life and career will be the result of having insufficient or incorrect information. If you do not have the knowledge or information yourself, where can you get it? Is it a core skill or activity that you need to learn yourself through reading and study, or can you hire someone else with this knowledge? Can you employ someone temporarily, such as a consultant or a specialist with the knowledge you require? Who else has achieved success in your field? Could you go to him or her for advice? Make a list of all the information, talents, skills, abilities, and experience that you'll need, and then make a plan to acquire, buy, rent, or borrow this information or skill as quickly as you can.

Determine exactly the most important information that you lack. The old 80/20 rule may apply. Say 80 percent of the value of the information you need will be contained in 20 percent of the information available. What is the most important information or ability that you will require to achieve your goal?

Step Nine: List the People You'll Need

In order to accomplish anything worthwhile, you'll need the help and cooperation of many people. Step number nine in goal achieving is to *make a list of all the people whose help and cooperation you'll require.* It may include your family, your boss, your customers, your bankers, your business partners or sources of capital, and even your friends.

Then take this list and organize it in order of priority. Whose help is the most important? Whose help is the second most important? This brings us to the law of compensation, a corollary of the law of sowing and reaping: for every action, there's an equal and opposite reaction, and you're going to be compensated in kind for everything that you put in. This law also says that people will only help you if they feel that they'll be compensated for their efforts in turn. A key question for you, then, is, what are you going to do for them to get them to help you?

You must always tune in to each person's favorite radio station, WII-FM: *what's in it for me?* Social and business relations are based on the law of reciprocity, which says that people will be willing to help you achieve your goals because you've demonstrated a willingness to help them to achieve their goals. The most successful men and women are those who have systematically helped the greatest number of other people to advance.

The law of compensation leads to the law of overcompensation: the habit of always doing more than you're paid for. Successful people exceed expectations: they do more than is expected of them. The only part of the equation of compensation and reciprocity that you can control is the amount that you put into it, because this is part of the law of sowing and reaping. If you take every opportunity that you can to help others, others will eventually give you all the help that you require.

**Successful people exceed expectations:
they do more than is expected of them.**

Two other cosmic laws are important to consider when you are assessing the people, groups, and organizations whose cooperation you require: the *law of service* and the *law of return*. Again, these are subsidiaries of the law of cause and effect, of sowing and reaping. The law of service says that your rewards in life will always be equal to the value of your service to others. The law of return says that you'll always get back in like measure what you put in. If you put in hard work, helpfulness, and honesty, you'll get back riches, rewards, and the respect of other people. If you wish to increase the quantity and quality of your returns, increase the quality and quantity of your service.

After a lifetime of research into success, Napoleon Hill concluded that the principle of organized effort, of what he called a Master Mind—people working together toward mutually agreed upon goals—is the basis for all great accomplishment. An indispensable part of success is the willingness and ability to cooperate effectively with others to help them achieve their goals so that they'll help you to achieve yours.

Step Ten: Make a Plan

Step number ten is simply to *make a plan*. By writing out in detail what you want, when you want it, where you're starting from, the obstacles you must overcome, the information you require, and the people whose help you need, you have all the ingredients of a superb master plan for the achievement of your goal.

A plan is merely a list of activities organized by time and priority. A list organized on the basis of time starts with the first thing that you have to do, all the way through to the last thing that you need to do before your goal is achieved. You can work on many activities at the same time, although certain ones have to be done continuously, from the beginning through until the end.

A plan is a list of activities organized by time and priority.

A plan organized by priority lists activities in their order of importance. What is the most important thing to do? What is the second most important thing? Keep asking this question until you have listed every activity based on its value to the completed goal.

Some years ago, the chairman of a conglomerate offered me a rare opportunity. He'd been approached by a Japanese automobile manufacturing company and offered the distributorship for their vehicles for a large area. He asked me if I would like to evaluate the vehicles with a view toward taking on the distributorship, setting up dealerships, and importing and distributing the vehicles.

I recognized this as a chance for rapid advancement, and I immediately accepted. The problem was that I didn't have the slightest idea of where to start or what to do. I immediately went into the marketplace and did two solid months of research on the importation and distribution of Japanese automobiles. I visited every dealership selling similar cars. I asked everybody I could find for help and advice. As it happened, one of the businessmen that I spoke to had been hired four years before by a large corporation to do a complete feasibility study on automobile importation from Japan. Nothing had come of his study, but he still had all his notes. I asked him if I could look through his research files. Among the materials that he showed me, I found a list of forty-five steps. This list had been compiled based on years of experience and months of research on the forty-five things that a person had to do in order to set up a dealership network and import and distribute Japanese vehicles to that network.

I got a copy of the list from him, and I began with number one. I carried the list with me day and night. Three months later, I had completed every item on the list, and the first vehicles rolled off the ship from Japan. We went on to sell $25 million worth of vehicles and earn millions of dollars in profits, because I had the list. This is just another example of how much you can accomplish starting from wherever you are if you have a good enough plan and a good enough list properly organized.

Once you have a detailed plan of action, get started. Be prepared to accept that your plan will have defects and flaws in it. It will not be perfect the first time out. Superior men and women can accept feedback as valuable information and change their plans to fit reality as they find it. Keep working on your plan until you have all the bugs out. Each time you hit a roadblock or an obstacle, go back and review your plan and make the necessary corrections. Eventually you'll have a plan that will work for you like a well-oiled machine. The more detailed and better organized your plans, the more likely you are to achieve your goals on schedule and exactly as you have defined them.

Keep working on your plan until you have all the bugs out.

Step Eleven: Visualization

Step number eleven in goal attainment is *visualization*. Create a clear mental picture of your goal as already achieved, and replay this picture over and over again on the screen of your mind. Every time you visualize your goal, you increase your desire and intensify your belief that you can achieve the goal. What you see is what you get: your subconscious mind is activated by pictures. All your goal setting and planning up to this point have been to give you an absolutely clear picture to feed systematically and continuously into your subconscious mind, like a series of commands that concentrates your mental powers and activates the law of attraction.

Step Twelve: Never Give Up

Step number twelve, the final step in achieving your goals, is to decide in advance that you will never give up. Back your goals and your plans with persistence and determination. Never consider the possibility of failure. Be like a bulldog; get your teeth into your goal and hold on, no matter what happens. As long as you refuse to quit, you will eventually be successful.

The Continuous Action Technique

Now that you have your goals and your plans, and you've decided that nothing's going to stop you until you've achieved success, use what I call the CAT, the *continuous action technique.* It will ensure that you stay on track toward your goal. It's based on the physical principle of momentum, which says that a body in motion tends to remain in motion unless acted upon by an outside force. It also says that it takes several units of energy to get a body from a resting position to a state of forward motion, but then it only takes one unit of energy to keep it in motion at the same speed. This is also called the principle of inertia, and you can use it to your advantage.

The principle of momentum also has mental and emotional and spiritual dimensions. It's the feeling of continuous motivation and excitement that you experience as you move progressively, step by step, toward the achievement of a worthy ideal or goal. Once you get started, the maintenance of momentum is critical to success. Many people launch themselves toward a goal and then allow themselves to come to a halt. Once you've stopped, getting yourself going again is sometimes so difficult that it never happens.

You maintain momentum by planning continuous action toward goal attainment. You define your goals in terms of the activities necessary to accomplish them. Then you discipline yourself to do something every day to move you toward the achievement of your major definite purpose. There's an old saying, "Nothing succeeds like success." You develop the success habit by achieving a win, even a small win, every single day.

You begin every day by reviewing your goals and committing yourself to doing something, anything, that moves you toward them. It may be something minor or it may be something major, but in order to maintain momentum and keep yourself positive and motivated, you must be continually taking actions consistent with what you hope to achieve.

Begin every day by reviewing and committing yourself to your goals.

Use the continuous action technique every day until you become a perpetual-motion goal setting and goal achieving human being. Make sure that each day is marked by an accomplishment of some kind, preferably first thing in the morning, to get your day started right. Fast tempo is essential to success. The more things you do and try and the faster you try them, the more energy and enthusiasm you'll have and the more you'll accomplish.

Here's an action exercise for you: Take your major definite purpose and go step by step through the goal setting methodology I've just explained. If you don't have a major definite purpose, make it your major definite purpose to find your major definite purpose, using the same methodology. Can you have more than one major definite purpose? Can you ride two bicycles at the same time? Absolutely not. More than one major definite purpose is no major definite purpose.

To complete this exercise, once you've worked out a complete detailed plan of action for your major definite purpose, do the same for one goal in each of your physical, mental, material, family, community, and spiritual areas. Put yourself on the high road to success through systematic goal setting and goal planning, and you will never look back.

Major Points

- A burning desire for achievement overcomes inertia.
- Setting believable goals is key to reaching them.
- Write down your goals to make them concrete in your mind.
- To accomplish anything worthwhile, you'll need the help of many people.
- Successful people do more than is expected of them.
- Keep working on your plan until you have all the bugs out.

SIX

The Superconscious:
The Secret of the Ages

This book is designed as a series of lessons in sequence, with each one building on the one before. Having read so far, you'll have become a far more thoughtful person than you were before. Your ability to use your mind in a constructive way will have increased dramatically. You've learned how to apply certain mental laws to help you get more of what you want in life. You understand the role of your self-concept and how your inner attitudes of mind shape the outer aspects of your reality. You've now accepted full responsibility for the person you are and everything you become. You now understand the importance of clear, specific goals, and you should have made a complete detailed plan for what you want to do and have and become over the next two to five years. You have begun systematically and continuously programming your subconscious mind with your goals and aspirations so that they'll appear more rapidly in your world. You're already becoming a more positive and optimistic person, and you're developing greater confidence in your ability to achieve your goals and objectives.

Now you're ready to learn the secret of the ages. It has been lost and found and lost again throughout history. It is simply this: *you have available to you a power and an intelligence which, when properly used, will enable you to solve any problem, overcome any obstacle, and achieve any goal that you sincerely desire long enough and hard enough.* Many of the greatest thinkers who have ever lived have stood in awe before this power and have written about it, calling it many different names. Poet and philosopher Ralph Waldo Emerson called it the "Oversoul," and he said, "We lie in the lap of an immense intelligence that responds to our thought."

Emerson compared this intelligence to an ocean and said that when we receive insights from it, we recognize them as coming from far beyond ourselves and our own limited minds. Napoleon Hill referred to this power as "infinite intelligence," calling it the universal storehouse of knowledge and the source of all imagination and creativity. He claimed that the ability to access this intelligence was a central part of the great success enjoyed by the hundreds of wealthy men and women he studied. Carl Jung, the Swiss psychologist and psychoanalyst, called it the "collective unconscious," and he felt that it contained within it all the wisdom of the human race, past, present, and future. It's also been called the universal subconscious mind, or the Universal Mind. Many people refer to it as the God Mind or the creative subconscious. I prefer simply to call it the *superconscious mind.* Whatever you choose to call it, there's no limit to what you can accomplish when you start tapping into it, using it, and letting it use you on a regular basis.

**Infinite intelligence is the universal storehouse
of knowledge and the source of all creativity.**

It would be difficult to explain how the superconscious mind works if you weren't already familiar with it, but throughout your life, you've used it many times in a random and haphazard fashion. In fact, much of what you've already accomplished can be attributed to your accidental use of this power. My purpose here is to show you how to use this power in a systematic way to dramatically increase the quality and quantity of the happiness and prosperity that is available to you.

The superconscious mind is the source of all pure creativity. All great classical art, music, and literature come from the superconscious. Emerson confessed that his essays seemed to write themselves. He would sit down at his desk and the words would simply pour through him onto the paper. His essays still read as some of the most beautiful and inspiring writing in the English language. Mozart was composing music at a young age. He could see and hear the music in his mind and was able to write it down note-perfect the first time. In the movie *Amadeus*, Salieri, a composer who is jealous of Mozart, says, "He writes the most beautiful music in the world as though he were taking dictation." Beethoven, Bach, Brahms, and Stravinsky all accessed this mind when composing their greatest pieces of music. Whenever you hear a piece of music, see a work of art, or read a piece of writing that seems timeless and touches something deep inside you, you are experiencing a superconscious creation.

The superconscious mind is also responsible for technological inventions and breakthroughs. Thomas Edison regularly tapped his superconscious mind to find the solutions that led to his hundreds of successful inventions. Nikola Tesla, perhaps the greatest electrical genius of his age, was able to construct models of electric motors in his mind, mentally disassemble them, reassemble them, and repair them until they were perfect. He would then go into a workshop and build a totally new machine or motor that would work perfectly the very first time.

The superconscious mind is also the source of all inspiration and motivation as well as the excitement that you feel when things are going really well for you. It's the source of hunches, intuition, the still small voice within, and flashes of insight. Whenever you've been wrestling with a problem and have suddenly experienced a great idea that turns out to be the perfect solution, you've been tapping into your superconscious mind.

Every time you've had a burst of spontaneous creativity that's given you a new answer, a new insight, into a challenge you were facing, your superconscious mind was working. When your super-conscious mind computes a problem or works on a goal, it has access to all the information stored in your subconscious mind, to every bit of information that you've ever taken in.

Every time you've had a burst of spontaneous creativity, your superconscious mind was working.

The superconscious mind can also discriminate between valid and invalid information. Each person has stored in his or her sub-conscious memory bank an enormous amount of information that is simply not true. Some of it is important and some of it is unimportant, but in all cases, the superconscious mind uses only the information that is true and accurate. It therefore brings you answers and solutions that are perfectly appropriate to your situation. Sometimes you get an idea that seems inconsistent with what you think you know to be true. Then it will turn out that your knowledge was incomplete or based on false information. The seemingly contradictory idea or solution will turn out to be the correct one.

The superconscious mind has access to knowledge and information outside and beyond your personal experience. This is because it actually lies outside the brain. It lies outside the conscious and subconscious mind of the individual. On one famous occasion, the Englishman Michael Faraday, who was not trained as a scientist, awoke in the middle of the night to find his mind teaming with scientific formulations. He wrote down several pages of mathematical formulas and scientific calculations that seemed to flow through him like a river of energy. Once he had finished writing, he fell back asleep, exhausted. When he took his notes to one of the most learned men in England, it was determined that he had produced knowledge that had never before existed. Faraday's work laid the foundation for the development of the vacuum tube and the entire electronic age in which we now live, and it came from the superconscious mind.

The superconscious mind has access to knowledge and information beyond your personal experience.

It's as though we are surrounded by a universal mind that contains all the intelligence, ideas, and knowledge that has ever existed or ever will exist. Often different people in different parts of the world will come up with the same ideas at the same time. One of our seminar graduates worked with a team at the Atomic Energy Research Council of Canada to develop a gamma ray back flash measuring device. It took them two years to perfect the device, but the key was an insight that this individual had had while working on the project. Some months later, at an international symposium that included scientists from the Soviet Union, where everyone's research was shared, they found that a Soviet scientist had had exactly the same insight at almost exactly the same time, and it led to the Soviets developing almost exactly the same device. Since both of these projects were top secret before being shared publicly, there was no way the information could have been exchanged through any other medium except the superconscious mind.

Once you begin using your superconscious capabilities in a systematic way, you'll start to get ideas that seem to be outside your current knowledge and experience. You've probably had the experience of thinking of a good idea for a new product or service, dismissing it because it was in a field in which you had no experience, and seeing some other company come out with the same product or service a couple of years later and make a fortune. The difference between the person who had the idea and ignored it and the one who had the idea and ran with it was that the latter had a higher level of trust and confidence in himself and in his ability to turn the idea into reality.

You often ignore your own ideas, falsely assuming that they couldn't be worth very much. This is the result of childhood conditioning. As soon as you begin accepting your creative powers and your superconscious capabilities, you will be amazed at ideas that come to you, and this time you'll do something about them.

Your superconscious mind functions on an unconscious level twenty-four hours per day, 365 days per year. Once you've programmed a goal or a problem into your subconscious mind and released it, it is transferred to your superconscious computer, which goes to work on it. You can then go about your daily life with your conscious and subconscious energies focused on the work at hand, while your superconscious mind is busily computing and preparing to bring you the answer you need. The conscious mind identifies, analyzes, decides, and commands. The subconscious mind stores and retrieves information and obeys the commands of the conscious mind. The superconscious mind functions outside and beyond both of them but is accessed through them.

Your superconscious mind functions on an unconscious level twenty-four hours per day, 365 days per year.

Activating the Superconscious

Your superconscious mind is capable of goal-oriented motivation. It is the source of the enthusiasm and excitement that you feel when you begin setting and accomplishing goals. However, to generate this motivation, your superconscious requires clear, specific goals to which you are completely committed. It will then release ideas and energy for attaining that goal. Your superconscious mind is a source of free energy; this is the mental and physical energy that you tap into during periods of great excitement, intense desire, or even extreme danger. When you're working towards something that's important to you, you often experience a boundless flow of energy that enables you to work day and night with very little sleep. Usually this is called nervous energy, but the nerves have no energy of their own.

Have you ever had the experience of having to get up in the middle of the night because of an emergency to find yourself wide awake, alert, and functioning effectively, whereas just a short while before you were very tired and sound asleep? This is an example of tapping into the free energy of the superconscious.

When you become fully attuned to your superconscious mind, you'll find yourself with a continuous flow of health, energy, and strength that will enable you to produce more in a few hours than the average person produces in a week. You will enter regularly into *flow*, a state in which the world seems to slow down while your mind seems to speed up. During this time, you have the capacity to produce enormous quantities of work almost effortlessly, and you have a wonderful sense of well-being. Your mind will sparkle with a steady stream of ideas that seem to be available to you exactly as you need them.

The superconscious mind responds best to clear, authoritative commands or positive affirmations. Every time you affirm a goal or a desire from your conscious mind to your subconscious mind, you activate your superconscious mind to release the ideas and energy that you need to bring your desire into reality. This is why decisiveness is such an important trait of successful men and women. When you stop vacillating and make a clear, unequivocal decision that you're going to do something, no matter what the cost, everything suddenly starts to work in your favor. When you say things such as, "I like myself," or "I can do it," or "I weigh a certain number of pounds," or "I earn X number of dollars per year," you are throwing the master switch on all your mental powers. When you do, you'll continually amaze yourself and others.

People fail to achieve their potential principally because they're simply not serious: they refuse to make the decisions that they must make if their lives are going to change for the better.

You'll be amazed at how much more effective you become when you make firm decisions and burn your metal bridges behind you. Cut off all thought of quitting, retreating, or doing something else. Decide that you are going to do whatever it takes to achieve your goal and that nothing is going to stop you. At that point, even an average mind becomes an extraordinary tool of accomplishment. Your superconscious mind automatically and continuously solves every problem on the way to your goal—as long as your goal is clear. If your goal is to make a lot of money and you're absolutely clear about the amount you wish to earn and keep, you will eventually reach your goal.

The history of the human race is written in the life stories of men and women who have set big, exciting goals for themselves and who have then persisted indomitably, sometimes for many years, and finally reached them. Peter Drucker, author of *The Effective Executive*, says that whenever you find something getting done anywhere, you'll find a monomaniac with a mission. Whenever you find great achievement, you find an individual who is absolutely clear about what he or she wants to do and who is willing to do whatever it takes for however long it takes.

Great achievement comes from individuals who are clear about what they want to do and are willing to do whatever it takes.

Your job is to keep your eye on the ball, to keep your mind on the goal. When you do, your superconscious mind will automatically and continuously solve each problem on the way to your goal. The Bible says, "Take . . . no thought for the morrow: for the morrow shall take thought for the things of itself. Sufficient unto the day is the evil thereof" (Matthew 6:34). In a way, this means that you can absolutely trust this superconscious power to function for you when and as you require it, and not before.

Your superconscious mind operates best in a mental climate of faith and acceptance, of confident expectations. Confidently expecting that your problems will be solved, your obstacles removed, and your goals achieved intensifies the rate of vibration of thought and causes your superconscious mind to function at its maximum. Although this is difficult to do initially, it's only when you're completely relaxed about the outcome of any situation that it seems to resolve itself, sometimes in the most unexpected way. Nevertheless, the outcome will always be everything that you could ask for and sometimes much more. The harder you *don't* try, the more that you practice letting go, the more of this superconscious power is available to you.

All great men and women have been people of faith. They have had the ability to trust themselves, in an almost childlike way, to the goodness of the universe, with the simple faith that everything was unfolding as it should at its own time. Most other people, however, are impatient and demanding; their very irritation causes negative emotions that shut off the superconscious mind and make its powers unavailable to them.

The Experiences You Need

The superconscious mind brings you the experiences you need to be successful. Because you can never permanently achieve anything on the outside that you are not fully prepared for on the inside, when you set a goal for yourself, you'll have to learn and grow and change to be ready to achieve it. Since we only really learn through experience (usually difficult and challenging experience), the superconscious mind will teach you the lessons that you need to learn so that when you finally arrive at your destination, it'll almost seem like an anticlimax. You will by then have developed the mental equivalent of the corresponding outer reality that you desire.

This is a very important point. If you achieve any level of accomplishment without having prepared for it mentally, you will not be able to hold on to it. If you make a lot of money unexpectedly and your self-concept is not equal to it, you'll be subconsciously driven to engage in behaviors to get rid of the money. This is why they say, "Easy come, easy go." But if you achieve your success slowly and gradually, growing as a person as you grow in productive capacity, when you finally reach the position you desire, you'll be ready to keep it indefinitely. If you look back over your life, you will find that almost everything that you have accomplished was preceded by what appeared to be difficulties, disappointments, and temporary failure. Often you've had to ride an emotional roller coaster of fear, anxiety, and worry. But when you look back, you can see that every one of those apparently negative experiences was essential to your achieving your ultimate goal and getting to where you are today.

If you achieve any accomplishment without having prepared for it mentally, you will not be able to hold on to it.

Your superconscious mind sets up a series of hurdles or learning experiences that are meant to train you to be capable of winning through in the end. Your superconscious mind is also very patient. If you don't learn the lesson—whether it's in relationships, business, money, or health—your superconscious mind will send you back through the obstacle course and through the learning experiences over and over until you finally learn what you're meant to learn. Then and only then will you be allowed to proceed to the next step in your development.

Napoleon Hill found that almost every single one of the wealthy men that he interviewed had achieved their great success one step beyond what appeared to be their greatest failure. When every outward indication suggested that it was time to give up, they were the closest to breaking through to their goal. It's as though the superconscious mind gives you a final test just before you arrive at your destination. When you're going through your most difficult learning experiences, you must draw on your ability to control your mind. You must have faith that the difficulties are simply part of the process that will inevitably bring you through to achieving your goal.

Successful men and women never use the word *failure*. They look upon a temporary defeat or setback as simply another way of learning how to succeed. Within every obstacle or disappointment, they seek the seed of an equal or greater benefit. They learn from every experience, but most of all, they keep their minds calm, positive, and focused on the goal. So keep your mind positive and your superconscious capabilities switched on.

Synchronicity and Serendipity

There's a phenomenon in human experience called *synchronicity*. Synchronicity occurs when two seemingly unrelated events occur at the same time, and coincidentally, both of these events help you to move toward one of your goals. For example, you could think about taking a vacation to Hawaii in the morning before you go to work, and later on that day receive a special offer for a week in Hawaii at a cut-rate price. Or you might decide over the weekend that you need to be earning more money, and Monday your boss could offer you a promotion with greater responsibilities and higher pay. The only connecting link between these synchronous events is the meaning imposed upon the events by your mind and your goal. This is another form of superconscious activity. Another word that is often used to describe this kind of coincidence is *serendipity.* Serendipity is the activity of making happy discoveries.

People who experience serendipity all seem to have one thing in common: they are all actively seeking something. They all seem to have clear goals, and the remarkable things they find are all associated with something they want to accomplish. People frequently tell me after they've started using their superconscious minds, "You won't believe what happened to me." I've heard this exclamation a thousand times.

Other people, even when it happens to them, will tend to dismiss these seemingly inexplicable coincidences by calling them luck or accident. But we live in a universe that's governed by law. Nothing happens by chance. Everything happens as the result of definite laws and principles, even if we cannot clearly identify them at the time.

Your superconscious mind operates best under two conditions: (1) when your conscious mind is concentrating 100 percent on the problem or goal, or (2) when your conscious mind is concentrating on something else altogether. You should try both methods on any problem.

A Five-Step Process

Here is a simple five-step process for bringing all the powers of your conscious mind to bear on a single problem.

1. Define the problem or goal clearly, preferably in writing.
2. Gather as much information as you can. Read, research, ask questions, and actively seek for the answer that you need.
3. Consciously try to solve the problem by reviewing all the information that you gathered.

4. If you still haven't been able to solve the problem consciously, turn it over to your superconscious mind. Simply release it confidently, the way you would release a helium balloon and let it float away.

5. Get your mind busy elsewhere.

Take any problem that you're wrestling with right now, and try this method on it. You may be amazed at the results. Your superconscious mind will bring you exactly the right answer for you at exactly the right time. When the answer comes, you must act on it immediately. It is time-dated material. If you get the urge to telephone someone or say or do something and it feels exactly right, act in faith and follow your instincts, because it will almost always turn out to be the right thing to do. If you're having a problem with another person and you get a clear idea of what you should do or say, even if it involves some confrontation or unpleasantness, follow your hunch and carry through with it. In my experience, the outcome will always be equal to or better than you could have expected.

The Law of Superconscious Activity

This brings us to the most important law that I will discuss here. It's called the *law of superconscious activity*. It says that any thought, goal, plan, or idea held continuously in the conscious mind, whether positive or negative, must be brought into reality by the superconscious mind. As I've already said, you create your world by the quality, quantity, and emotional intensity of the thoughts that you allow to dominate your thinking. If you keep your mind continuously on things you want and keep it off of things you fear, eventually your goals will materialize and become your reality.

Any thought, goal, or idea held continuously in the conscious mind must be brought into reality by the superconscious mind.

Like all the other laws, this law is neutral. It is no respecter of persons. It is the highest manifestation of the principle of cause and effect. If you use this power for good, then only good will come into your life. If you use this power negatively, it'll bring you illness, unhappiness, and financial difficulties. The choice is always up to you. You are always free to choose the kind of world that you wish to live in. You become what you think about. A successful life is merely a series of successful days, hours, and minutes in which you think and talk about your goals and desires about health, happiness, and prosperity and refuse to dwell on anything that you don't want.

There are several ways to stimulate superconscious activity. The most predictable and dependable is simply to think about your goals all the time. This alone will keep your mind positive and will cause your superconscious energies to flow through you in the form of ideas and motivation toward their achievement.

The next most powerful way to stimulate your superconscious mind is through solitude: going into the silence. When I read the lives of great men and women, I find that almost invariably they begin to become great when they begin to take time to be alone with themselves. Solitude is a wonderful tonic that gives balance and clarity to thought. Solitude provides an opportunity for you to reflect on who you are and what's important to you. Most of all, solitude provides the mental medium of calmness and serenity that causes superconscious solutions to spring into your mind, full-blown and complete in every detail.

If you've never practiced solitude, simply sit somewhere perfectly silently, without moving, for an entire hour. Do not drink coffee, take notes, smoke cigarettes, listen to music, or do anything else. Simply sit perfectly still for an entire hour. If you've never done this before, you'll find it to be excruciatingly difficult. For the first twenty-five to thirty minutes, you will have an irresistible urge to get up and move around, but if you have the self-discipline to sit without moving for thirty minutes, a remarkable thing will happen. In almost every case, you'll start to feel calm, relaxed, and at peace with yourself and the world. Your mind will slow down and relax, and you'll feel a flow of energy entering your body from all sides. You'll feel happy and at one with the world. You'll be glad that you've taken this time, and you will recognize it as a valuable investment in your inner development.

Visualizing your ideal goal as if it were already realized is another way of triggering superconscious activity. Many people find that daydreaming or relaxing on a park bench triggers super-conscious activity. Listening to classical music, alone or in the company of people you enjoy, will often cause wonderful ideas to spring into your mind. Perhaps one of the most enjoyable ways to turn on your superconscious powers is to go for a walk or commune with nature. The sounds of the ocean on the seashore seem to have a powerful impact on the superconscious. Deep relaxation or meditation is also very helpful in stimulating your supercon-scious mind.

In our fast-paced life, the great danger to the person who wishes to achieve their full potential is a tendency to dismiss these ideas because they are too busy. But one good superconscious insight or idea can save you months and even years of hard work. It is exactly when you are too busy to stop that you need to stop most urgently.

The Superconscious Solution

A superconscious solution will come from one of three sources. The first and most frequent source is from intuition: the still, small voice within. Sometimes that inner voice will shout at you so loud that you will know that this is exactly the right thing for you to do. The best advice that I could ever give you is to always trust your intuition. Never go against your intuition: it is your direct pipeline to the superconscious mind and infinite intelligence. Men and women become great to the degree to which they listen to and trust their intuition.

The second source of superconscious solutions is chance encounters with other people or with information sources. Once you have a clear goal or a clear problem to solve on the way to your goal, you'll unexpectedly meet people who can help you. You'll come across books, magazines, and articles that contain exactly the information that you need.

Start off each morning by saying, "I believe something wonderful is going to happen to me today." If you go around believing that something wonderful is about to happen to you, you'll tend to meet people and come across information that will make your expectation a self-fulfilling prophecy.

The third source of superconscious solutions is unpredictable events. Peter Drucker says that the primary sources of innovation in business are the unexpected success and the unexpected failure. It's often the completely unanticipated event that contains the superconscious solution that you are seeking.

The unexpected event often appears to be a major setback or failure. Sir Alexander Fleming was conducting experiments at his laboratory in London when some mold flew onto his culture dishes and ruined the experiment. As he was about to throw away the culture medium and begin again, he noticed that the mold had killed the bacteria in the dishes. He began to study the mold and discovered penicillin, which won him a Nobel Prize in medicine and saved the lives of millions of men and women during World War II.

The inspirational author Norman Vincent Peale says, "Whenever God wants to send you a gift, he wraps it up in a problem or a difficulty. The bigger the problem you have, the bigger the potential gift." The question that separates the winners and losers is simply this: how are you going to respond to this situation? The winning human being always looks into even the most difficult situation for whatever good it may contain.

Characteristics of the Superconscious Solution

How do you tell a superconscious solution as opposed to a solution that may come from the conscious or subconscious mind? A superconscious solution has three characteristics.

1. When it comes, it is 100 percent complete and deals with every aspect of the problem. It is always within your resources and capabilities at the time. It is always simple and easy to implement.

2. It appears to be a blinding flash of the obvious. It seems to be so simple and evident that you often have the aha or the eureka reaction. You wonder why you hadn't thought of it before. It was either because you weren't ready or because the timing was not right.

3. A superconscious solution always comes accompanied by a burst of joy and energy, a feeling of elation that inspires you to act immediately. If you get a superconscious solution in the middle of the night, you'll be unable to sleep until you get up and write it down or do something about it.

**A superconscious solution is always
accompanied by a burst of joy and energy.**

There's the famous story of the Greek scientist Archimedes taking a bath and suddenly having the superconscious solution that enabled him to determine the quantity of gold in the king's crown. He became so excited that he ran through the streets of the city naked, shouting, "Eureka, eureka!" which is Greek for, "I have found it, I have found it!" When your superconscious solution comes to you, even after a long period of mental and physical work, you'll have that same feeling of excitement and joy and enthusiasm, and you'll be eager to rush out and put the solution into action.

All the powers of the human mind combine together in this marvelous law, which says that any thought plan, goal, or idea held continuously in the conscious mind, whether positive or negative, must eventually be brought into reality by the superconscious mind. When you have clearly defined goals, with detailed plans backed by an unshakably positive mental attitude and a calm, confident expectation of success, you will activate your superconscious mind into bringing you everything you could ever want in life.

An Action Exercise

Here's an action exercise for you: Schedule one hour of solitude during which you will go somewhere and sit perfectly still for sixty minutes. Make an appointment with yourself for one hour. Discipline yourself to do this as soon as possible. During this period of silence, you will get ideas and insights that will propel you toward your goal and may save you a lot of time and money.

Resolve to tune into and trust your superconscious mind continuously, listening for answers with calm, positive expectancy. Your superconscious mind will then guide and direct you to do and say the right things in every situation, and you'll begin to move ahead rapidly. Be sure that everything that you say and do is consistent with what you want and where you want to go. In no time at all, your life will start to take off, and you'll be on the high road to success and happiness. Go for it, and good luck.

Major Points

- You have available to you a power and intelligence that will enable you to achieve any goal: the superconscious mind.
- The superconscious mind responds best to clear, authoritative commands or positive affirmations.
- Faith, acceptance, and confident expectation enable your superconscious to work at its best.
- Active seeking activates synchronicity.
- Spending time in solitude is an excellent way to activate the superconscious.

SEVEN

Time Management

One of the most important skills to learn in order to achieve everything you are capable of is time management. Time management, which is really life management, is the core skill around which everything else revolves. Indeed the quality of your life is determined by the quality of your time management. No other skill can give you a greater payoff in rewards, happiness, increased effectiveness, and the pleasure of knowing that you can achieve your goals.

Time management is a skill, just like typing or riding a bicycle: it can be learned with practice and repetition. You can use time management as a tool to build a great life and a great career. You can see it as a vehicle, like a bus, which you can take to get from wherever you are to wherever you want to go. All effective men and women are experts at time management. In fact, the further up you move on the ladder of success, the more likely you are to excel at organizing and using your time in the most effective way.

All effective men and women are experts at time management.

Time management is the external demonstration of self-discipline: every single act strengthens your character and increases your ability to achieve your goals that are important to you. Conversely, every incident of slacking off will undermine your effectiveness, lower your self-esteem, and interfere with your goal-achieving capacity.

One quality of the most successful men and women in America is intense result orientation. Your rewards, both tangible and intangible, will be determined by the quality and the quantity of the results that you get for yourself and others. Everything you do that increases your ability to achieve important results will increase the likelihood that you become wealthy during your career.

**Your rewards will be determined by the
quality and quantity of your results.**

Some people say they don't have the time for all the things they need to do in order to be successful. This is nonsense. You and I have all the time there is: twenty-four hours per day, seven days per week, 365 days per year. The only question is how we are going to deploy this resource. How can we organize ourselves so that we spend the maximum amount of time on our highest-value activities? The ability to organize your time and use it effectively will determine almost everything that you accomplish.

Time is completely inelastic and inflexible. It cannot be stretched. The amount of time that you have is all there is, and you cannot get any more of it. Yet it is the one indispensable ingredient of achievement. No accomplishment is possible without an investment of time. It is irreplaceable, especially in relationships. There's no substitute for it. You cannot replace it with money, effort, knowledge, or skill. Time is required for anything you want to do or have or become.

Finally, time is perishable. It cannot be saved, preserved, or stored. Once it's gone, it's lost forever. It's like a hotel room: if it's not rented out tonight, it can't be saved for another time. The more seriously you look upon your time as an expression of yourself and your life, the more likely you are to excel at time management.

Good time management develops judgment, foresight, self-reliance, and courage, especially the courage to make hard choices among competing demands. These are also the essential qualities of leadership. They are necessary to enable you to get things done, by yourself and through others.

Utilizing your time well enables you to work smarter, not just harder. You probably know that many people who are failures work harder and longer hours than successful people. But they produce less, so they are paid less, because of poor personal management skills that cause them to end up working on lower-value tasks.

Good time management is a source of energy, enthusiasm, and a positive mental attitude. True motivation comes from a feeling of competence and mastery. When you're using your time in such a way that you're producing at your maximum capacity, you cannot help but feel terrific about yourself.

Time management begins with clear goals and objectives. The key word here is *clarity*. People frequently lose sight of what they started off to accomplish. They often work frantically to achieve things that they're unclear about. Perhaps the very worst use of time is to do something well that need not be done at all.

I've already talked about the importance of clarifying your values and your mission statement. From there, it's essential to write down your goals and organize them in order of priority and make action plans for their accomplishment, written out in detail. Once you have a clear blueprint for your life, you can organize every hour of every day for maximum efficiency. All you have to sell is your time. The way you plan and organize your time can have a greater impact on your health, wealth, and happiness than anything else you do.

Get Organized

The first thing to do before you can do any productive work is get yourself organized. The core function of good time management is planning and organizing yourself and your work for maximum productivity. The top 3 percent of achievers are persistent planners. They're forever writing and rewriting their lists of goals and subgoals. They think on paper, and they're continually analyzing and evaluating their plans, updating and improving them as they go along.

I used to wonder why so many successful people spent so much time planning. Over time, I learned that the more time you spend planning and reworking your plans, the better and more foolproof they become, and your goals become increasingly believable and achievable. You gain even more confidence in your ability to accomplish them.

When you break down even the biggest goal into its individual parts and then organize it into a step-by-step series of specific actions, it seems much more manageable. That's why the Chinese sage Lao-tzu said, "A journey of a thousand leagues begins with a single step." Once you've determined the first step, the second step follows naturally from that, and so on.

In addition, the more you plan, the deeper you program the goal into your subconscious mind, where it takes on a motivational power of its own, driving you forward. The payoff from good planning is enormous. It's estimated that one minute in planning saves at least five minutes in execution. Put another way, your investment in planning pays you a 500 percent return. Since all you have to sell is your time, the more productive and efficient your time usage (all other things being equal), the more you will eventually be paid. Where else can you get a 500 percent return on the investment of your time and energy?

Sometimes people say that they don't have time to sit and plan. The fact is that even if you force yourself, it's hard to spend more than a few minutes a day in planning, and the only way that you'll ever get the time you need is by planning your activities carefully in advance. This is the essence of self-discipline in time management; it is the essential starting point of success.

By contrast, action without planning is the reason for every failure. If you look back over the major mistakes that you've made in your life, they will almost all have one thing in common: you probably rushed into the situation without thinking about it enough. You either didn't get enough information, or you didn't take the time to weigh and balance the pros and cons before acting. You probably didn't take the time to plan carefully enough in advance. The old adage says, "A stitch in time saves nine."

You'll also find that each of your most successful accomplishments was accompanied by a good plan. The more time you took to think through the ramifications of your actions, the more efficient were your actions and the more satisfying the end result.

**Each of your most successful accomplishments
was accompanied by a good plan.**

The better and more complete your plans, the greater the likelihood of success. Someone once said that success is tons of discipline. One of the best exercises of self-discipline is to take the time to think through and plan out everything you do before you begin. Here are four ideas that you can use to help you master your time and get yourself organized.

Neatness Counts

First, neatness is essential for high levels of productivity. You can dramatically increase your productivity simply by cleaning up and organizing your workspace more effectively.

There's a saying that order is heaven's first law. Order is earth's first law too. You need a sense of order to feel relaxed and in control. You get a feeling of pleasure and satisfaction each time you put some part of your life or work in order. When you clean up your desk or office, when you clean out your car, when you organize your purse or your briefcase, your home or your closets, you feel like a more effective human being. You get a surge of energy and enthusiasm that makes you want to go on to some other task.

One good exercise is to stand back from your desk and ask what kind of a person works there. Look in your purse or briefcase and ask what kind of a person would have a purse or briefcase like that. Look at your car, look in your closet, look at your house and your yard, and ask what kind of a person would live that way. What does your environment say about you as a person? What signal does it send to other people about your competence, efficiency, and effectiveness? Looking at your work environment as if you were looking through the eyes of an objective third party, ask yourself, would I entrust a person whose work environment looks like that with an important task? Why or why not? Stand back and honestly evaluate yourself as if through the eyes of your boss or a neutral observer. What do you see? How could you improve the perception that another person might have of you from looking at your work environment?

In a recent series of interviews, fifty out of fifty-two executives said they would not promote a person with a messy desk or workplace, even if the person was producing good work and doing a good job. They said that they would not entrust a position of responsibility to a person who did not look well organized.

Many people who work in a messy environment or keep a messy desk use their intelligence to justify themselves. They say things like, "I know where everything is," or they say humorous things like, "A clean desk is a sign of a sick mind." However, every motion study of efficiency in the workplace has concluded that these are really exercises in self-deception. The people who say that they know where everything is are using too much of their mental capacity, their random-access memory, simply for remembering where they put things rather than doing the job.

People who say that they work well in a cluttered environment are usually wrong. If they worked in a neat, well-organized environment for any length of time, they would be surprised at how much more productive they would be. If you or a person you know justifies a cluttered desk, challenge yourself or the other person to work with a clean desk for one full day. The result will probably prove the point beyond the shadow of a doubt. Clear your desk of everything but the one thing that you are working on. If necessary, place things in drawers, on the credenza behind you, in the waste basket, in cupboards, or even on the floor. Do whatever is necessary to turn your desk into a clear, clean, uncluttered work environment with just one thing—the most important task in front of you—before you begin.

Before You Start

The second idea for getting yourself organized follows from the first: have everything you need at hand before beginning. Like a good cook, a master craftsman, or any professional, assemble all the tools of your trade before starting on the job. Get all the information that you'll need. Assemble the necessary files on your computer and smartphone. Get pens, papers, stick-on notes, calculator, ruler, phone, file folders, and anything else you will need. Your aim is to be able to sit down and do the entire job without getting up if you so desire. If you work out of a briefcase, the same rule holds true. Have everything you need at your fingertips.

Assemble all the tools of your trade before starting on the job.

The third idea to help you get organized is to resolve to handle every piece of paper (and, we could add today, each piece of email) only once. Decide to do something with it when you pick it up, and don't pick it up unless you're ready to act on it. It's better to stack it up and put it aside for appropriate action later than to keep picking it up and putting it down without taking any action.

The TRAF System

In her book *Getting Organized*, Stephanie Winston recommends the TRAF system to deal with paperwork. Each letter in the word TRAF stands for a specific action.

The letter T stands for *toss*. One of the best time management tools is the wastebasket. The fastest way to save time on reading anything is to simply throw it away. This applies to junk mail, unwanted subscriptions and catalogs, sales circulars, and anything else that's not relevant. Get rid of reading materials that have been hanging around for months. Ask yourself, "If I did not read this, would there be any negative consequences?" If the answer is no, throw it away as fast as you can. Restrain your curiosity about everything that comes to you in the mail. This alone can save you an enormous amount of time.

The next letter in the TRAF system is R, which stands for *refer*, or delegate. When you pick up a piece of paper or open an email, before doing anything with it, ask yourself if someone else should be acting on it. Is there someone else who can do it better than you? Is there anyone else to whom you can delegate action? If you're an executive with a staff, use the 70 percent rule: "Is there anyone else who can do this 70 percent as well as me?" If there is, then delegate it to that person. You must delegate every single thing that anyone else can possibly do if you're going to have enough time to do the few things that are most important. Pass off the task at the beginning rather than sitting with it and going back to it several times. It's amazing how much you'll save by taking this simple action of referring or delegating.

The third letter in the TRAF system is A, for *action*. These are the emails, letters, proposals, and other items that you personally must do something about. Open a folder on your computer desktop entitled "Action." Get a file folder and write the word "Action" on the tab. Have these folders handy. When you come across something that you need to act on, put it in these folders to work on later. In this way, at least you'll have made a decision on that item and moved it one step forward toward resolution.

The last letter is F, which stands for *file*. Before you file anything, electronically or on paper, remember that 80 percent of papers filed are never needed, used, or seen again. Designating something to be filed creates work for someone else. Before you decide to put something in your files, ask, what would happen if I couldn't find this item? What would be the negative consequences of not being able to have this information available? If there are no negative consequences or very few, or if you could get the information somewhere else, throw the piece of paper away. Simplify your life whenever possible.

The purpose of this TRAF system is to take action, any action, on any email that comes your way or piece of paper that you pick up. Do something, anything, with each item; move it along at least one step. One of the greatest time wasters is continually reading the same item, putting it down, and having to come back to it over and over again.

When You're Finished

The fourth idea for getting yourself organized is, when you're finished with something, put it away, and complete your transactions. Start with a clean workspace and end with a clean workspace. There is something deeply satisfying about task completion, and that means leaving nothing lying around.

Finish what you start. Encourage others to finish their work and put things away. Set a good example for your children, staff, and coworkers by putting things away as you go along. It's hard for most people to learn this habit, but it's one that serves them all their lives.

Time Management Tools

In addition to what we've discussed so far, there are several time management tools and procedures that you need to have to achieve maximum productivity. The first of these is some kind of time planning system, which contains everything you need to plan and organize every area of your life.

The best time planners enable you to plan for the year, for the month, for the week, and for each day and hour. The first requirement in your time planner is a master list, where you can write down every task, goal, or required action as it comes up. The master list becomes the core of your system. From this master list, you allocate individual tasks to various months, weeks, and days. With a master list, you can capture every duty, task, and responsibility and write it down without having to worry about remembering it later.

The second part of your time planning system should be calendars that enable you to lay out your time and plan your activity several months and weeks ahead. With the ideal system, you'll be able to transfer individual items from your master list to the month, week, and day when you intend to do them.

The third part of your time planning system should be a daily list. This daily list is perhaps the single most important planning tool. Some people call it a to-do list. Alan Laken, the time management expert, found that every effective executive he spoke with used this kind of list. He also found that ineffective people—those who felt swamped by too many things to do and too little time—not only did not use a list, but often resisted the idea of writing everything on a list before they began.

The daily to-do list is perhaps the single most important planning tool.

One myth of time management is that structuring your time and working from a list somehow limits your freedom and spontaneity. Exactly the opposite is true. The more things you organize and plan for, the more freedom you have and the more spontaneous you can be in other areas.

On your daily list, write down every single thing that you intend to do over the course of the day. My experience has proven that you can increase your productivity by 25 percent the very first day that you start using a list.

If you're not using one already, you can bring order out of chaos faster with a list than with any other time management tool. In fact, at any time you feel yourself overwhelmed with work, stop and take the time necessary to list every single thing you need to do. The very act of organizing your tasks and responsibilities on a list will enable you to bring them under your control. And remember, a feeling of control goes hand in hand with a heightened sense of well-being and inner peace.

During the course of the day, new tasks and responsibilities will come up. Telephone calls will have to be returned; correspondence will have to be dealt with. Discipline yourself to write every item down on the list before you do it. Something that seems urgent, something that would distract you from your work, often reveals its real significance when it's written down. Often something that's written on a list next to all your other tasks and responsibilities doesn't seem so important at all.

The ABCDE System

The next step in time management is to organize your list of the day's activities. The first key is to recognize the difference between the urgent and the important. Generally speaking, the urgent is seldom important, and the important is seldom urgent. The most pressing tasks on your list are those that are both urgent and important. They are in your face, they have to be done immediately, and they can have significant future consequences, positive or negative, if they are or are not completed.

The tasks or projects on your list that can have the greatest possible impact on your future are usually important, but not urgent. You'll find that organizing your time so you work more on these important but not urgent projects will give you the biggest payoffs in life satisfaction and career rewards.

The best way to organize your daily list is with the ABCDE system:

A stands for *must do, very important; serious negative consequences if not completed.*

B stands for *should do, important, but only minor negative consequences if not completed within a set period of time.*

C stands for *things that it would be nice to do, but they're not particularly important. No negative consequences would ensue if this were not done at all.*

D stands for *delegate.*

E stands for *eliminate.* Many tasks should be eliminated altogether because, although they may be enjoyable, they add very little to the value of your work.

In organizing your list with the ABCDE method, be sure to apply the 80/20 rule: 20 percent of what you do will account for 80 percent of your results on any given day. Look at your list and ask yourself, what are the one or two things that are probably more important than all the others put together? That is where you begin.

Condition yourself to use the list as your blueprint or roadmap for the day. This list is designed to show you how to get from the morning to the evening in the most efficient and productive way. The list is a guide to what you have to do and what is more or less important. Refuse to do anything until and unless you have written it down on the list and organized its value relative to the other items on your list.

Four Big Steps

In every area of endeavor, good work habits go hand in hand with success. Nothing will bring you to the attention of your superiors faster than developing a reputation for being a person with excellent work habits. How you work determines the quality and quantity of your rewards. It also determines how much you earn, how effective you are, how much you are respected in your organization, and how much real satisfaction you get from your job.

The foundation of good work habits can be summarized in two words: *focus* and *concentration. Focus* means clarity concerning the desired results and the relative priority of each step toward the results. When I think of focus, I think of a photographer adjusting the lens to keep the subject in sharp relief. To be truly effective at work, you have to be continually adjusting your lens so that what you're working on every minute is the most important thing you could be doing toward achieving your most important goals.

Concentration means being able to stay with the task until it is 100 percent complete. It means working in a straight line without diversion or distraction, without getting sidetracked into doing things of lesser importance.

Here are the big four steps to higher productivity, and they cannot be repeated too often.

1. Set clear goals and objectives in writing. Think them through carefully before you begin. What are you trying to do? How are you trying to do it? Whenever you experience frustration of

any kind, go back to these questions: "What am I trying to do?" "How am I trying to do it?"

2. The second step to higher productivity is a detailed plan of action for achieving your goals. This answers the question, "How am I trying to do it?" When you've clarified your goals and major plans, you'll have the answers to *what* and *how*—something that very few people ever take the time to think through.

3. The third step to higher productivity is establishing clear priorities: having your activities organized in a hierarchy of value and importance to your desired result. Apply the 80/20 rule over and over again, day by day, hour by hour, before you start any task or activity. The most important question of all in setting priorities is to ask yourself continually, "What is the most valuable use of my time right now?" Whatever the answer is to this question, anything else that you might do is a waste of time in comparison.

   To put it another way, ask yourself, "If I could only do one thing today before I was called away for a month, what would I do?" Once you've answered that, ask yourself, "If I could only complete one other thing before I was called away for a month, what would that be?"

   Another useful time management technique is to ask yourself, "What is the limiting step between where I am and where I want to go?" The limiting step is the bottleneck determining the speed at which you accomplish your goal or goals. For many people, their limiting step is their lack of knowledge of time management techniques. For one salesperson, the limiting step may be the number of prospects that he or she develops. For another salesperson, it may be the lack of closing techniques or having enough confidence to ask for the order at the end of the presentation. For many companies, the limiting step is the effectiveness of their advertising.

In almost every hour of every day, there's a limiting step that determines how fast you get the job done. Often removing your limiting step can be your highest priority—the most valuable thing that you can do at the moment.

Another key to discovering the most valuable use of your time right now is to choose the future over the past and ask yourself what action you could take that would have the greatest impact on your future. Usually the action that would have the greatest possible impact is the most important thing to do. Even though this task may not be not urgent, it is the most valuable use of your time. Completing a major proposal, for example, writing a book, or developing a new business plan may not be urgent, but the possible negative impact of its noncompletion could make it the most important thing to do.

Ask what action you could take that would have the greatest impact on your future.

---

4. The fourth step to higher productivity is concentrating single-mindedly on the task with the highest payoff. This is the real key to getting things done. Not completing or only partly completing major tasks is a major source of stress and is inherently demotivational. Furthermore, when you work on something that is unimportant, even if you do complete it in a timely fashion, you get no feeling of satisfaction or excitement.

By contrast, there are major benefits from concentrating on your highest-value tasks. As we've already seen, completion of an important task is a source of energy, enthusiasm, and self-esteem: when you accomplish it, you feel a burst of energy and elation; you feel motivated to do even more. It gives you a feeling of confidence, competence, personal mastery, as well as a feeling of self-control, a sense that you're in charge of your own destiny. The habit of completing your transactions, of finishing what you start, is also an essential part of character building. You cannot imagine yourself as a fully mature human being if you're unable to finish what you begin.

Visualization and Body Language

You can accelerate the process of becoming a highly productive person by visualizing yourself over and over as focused and channeled toward high achievement. See yourself as a highly productive, effective person. Imagine that you are already the person you want to be.

One powerful method of visualization is to think of an incident in your past when, for whatever reason, you forced yourself to concentrate on completing an important task. Now take that memory and replay it over and over again as you think of yourself today. Your subconscious mind records each replay of an emotionalized experience as though it were happening again in the present. If you repeatedly replay your previous experience of task completion on the screen of your mind, you'll eventually program your subconscious mind for greater concentration, and you'll find that it becomes easier and easier to stick with the job once you begin.

Another way to accelerate the process of becoming a highly productive person is to assume the body language of high performance. There is a body position or physiology for almost every mental and emotional state, including good work habits. If you work at a desk and you sit up straight and erect and lean forward, you trigger a feeling of greater productivity. If you walk briskly with your head up, your shoulders back, and your chin held high, you feel more like a confident and productive person. On the other hand, if you slouch in a chair, your productivity will decline; if you walk slowly with your head down, you'll feel a lack of self-confidence and a lack of enthusiasm for productive work.

Six Steps to Power Concentration

Here are six steps to developing the concentration that is common to all high-performing men and women.

1. Before you start to work, clear your workspace of everything except what you need to complete the highest priority task. Simplicity and order are more conducive to highly productive work than messiness and disorganization.

2. Plan your days and organize your work so that you create blocks of time. Find ways to rob time from other activities and consolidate it into blocks of a minimum of sixty to ninety minutes each. It's not possible to accomplish meaningful tasks in less time. By "meaningful tasks," I'm referring to creative work, such as reports and proposals, as well as discussions with and about people concerning their work, their lives, and the future of the organization. You cannot rush important conversations; you need to allow plenty of time for them to unfold and develop.

   By the way, if you put in 20 or 30 percent more time in an average day than your coworkers, you'll end up being paid double, triple, and quadruple what the average person is earning, simply by becoming marginally more productive. This is because the overall quality of your work will usually improve at the same rate as the quantity of your work improves.

Often big companies in large cities will rent an apartment near the office and furnish it with desks, chairs, and office supplies so that executives can go there and work without interruption away from telephones and drop-in visitors. Knowing that you won't be interrupted is conducive to better concentration and higher productivity.

There are three other ways you can accomplish greater quantities of work. The first is to come into the office a full hour before the workday begins. Often, you can clear up an entire day's work in that one hour. If you can't come in early, working straight through your lunch hour from twelve to one is a great time management technique. Almost everyone goes out to lunch at this time and the level of activity and telephone calls drops off dramatically. Take your lunch hour before twelve o'clock or after one o'clock. You can you get in and out faster, and you'll get better service and be back to work sooner than those who go to lunch at noon.

The third chunk of time that you can get during the workday is to stay for an hour or two after everyone has left. Many businesspeople, salespeople, and entrepreneurs find that this is the best way to stay on top of their jobs.

The key with regard to these sixty- to ninety-minute chunks of time is to take them completely without interruption. Close your door, unplug your telephone, stop checking your email, put your head down, and just work flat out. Very little productive work is done in an office environment with all the distractions of telephones and people coming and going.

Remember also that the last 20 percent of any conversation usually contains 80 percent of the value of that conversation. Similarly, the last 20 percent of these concentrated chunks of working time is generally the most productive, because your mind is now totally into your task. It often takes a long time to settle down and start to really work productively.

3. The third step to developing the habit of concentration is to remember that hard-sustained concentrated effort is central to high productivity and successful achievement. Every great accomplishment in human history has been preceded by an extended period of single-minded concentrated effort for a long time—sometimes months, even years. Every great career achievement is preceded by countless hours of hard work that very few people ever see or appreciate. It took Michelangelo many years to paint the Sistine Ceiling. When you think of any work of art or anything of lasting value, you recognize the perseverance and concentration that was necessary to create it. It's the same with your career.

4. The fourth step in enhancing concentration is to develop a compulsion to closure and an urge to completion. You do this by creating a reward system for the completion of a major task and refusing to give yourself a reward until the job is 100 percent complete. If you can involve someone else in the reward, like going out for dinner, taking a trip, or buying a new car, this will act as an added source of motivation. You need to give yourself a series of rewards for the completion not only of major tasks but of each important step along the way. You can train your subconscious mind to motivate you to continuous action by simply giving yourself rewards on a regular and systematic basis.

5. The fifth step to developing concentration is to program yourself with commands so that you'll be unconsciously impelled to continue working and concentrating on your highest-priority task. Time management author John Molloy recommends developing a trigger phrase to use when your attention wanders and you are

distracted from your work. Perhaps the best trigger phrase is, "Back to work." Whenever you find yourself getting distracted, just say emphatically to yourself, "Back to work, back to work, back to work." You'll be surprised at how easy it is to return to your work and start concentrating again.

When you begin your workday at eight or nine o'clock, resolve that you will simply work all the time you work. For the entire day, you will do what you are being paid for. You will not socialize, fool around, pick up your laundry, call your friends, or do your grocery shopping. You will simply work all the time you work. A firm decision to do this will help you to develop concentration as fast as, or faster than, any other technique.

Work all the time you work.

---

6. The sixth step to developing the habit of concentration is what Alec Mackenzie, in his book *The Time Trap*, called "single handling." Single handling means that once you start a task, you resolve to stay with it until it's 100 percent complete. If you pick up a letter, begin a report or proposal, or initiate a sales call, you discipline yourself to stay with it until it's finished. This simple technique can increase your productivity by as much as 50 percent the first day you start using it. I've been amazed over the years at how effective this is.

Single handling also enables you to take advantage of the learning curve. When you do a group of similar tasks together, the amount of time it takes to do each subsequent task usually declines. If you have to do ten or twenty of the same type of tasks, such as writing letters, answering emails, or filling out reports, the learning curve will enable you to decrease the time necessary for completing each one by as much as 80 percent. You become more efficient with every task that you perform, as long as you do them all together, one after the other.

Overcoming Procrastination

The final part of getting things done is overcoming procrastination. Procrastination is the thief of time and therefore the thief of life. It is the primary reason many people lead lives of quiet desperation and retire poor.

One way to overcome procrastination is to use the power of positive affirmation to program a sense of urgency into your subconscious mind. At the beginning of each task, repeat and affirm over and over the words, "Do it now. Do it now. Do it now." W. Clement Stone, who built an insurance fortune of more than $500 million, wrote that the repetition of the words, "Do it now," was a key factor in his rise from being a penniless boy selling newspapers on the streets of Chicago to becoming one of the richest men in America.

You can develop any mental habit you desire by repeated suggestions in the form of affirmations and mental pictures from your conscious mind to your subconscious mind. Eventually your subconscious mind will accept the command as the new operating instructions, and you'll find yourself with a sense of urgency that's as much of a habit as brushing your teeth and combing your hair.

Refuse to rationalize or make excuses for procrastination.

Procrastination is accompanied by rationalization, which is best defined as attempting to put a socially favorable interpretation on an otherwise socially unacceptable act. It's explaining away and making excuses for unproductive behavior. You'll notice that people who procrastinate always have what they think is a good reason.

Don't allow yourself the luxury of making excuses. Say you'll do it, and then burn your mental bridges. Refuse to consider the possibility of not doing it or the reason you're justified in putting it off.

There's a special technique you can use to overcome procrastination, and it is the use of creative procrastination: consciously deciding upon the things that you're going to procrastinate on. If you don't consciously decide to procrastinate on low-priority items, you'll invariably end up procrastinating on high-value tasks, because you never have enough time to do everything that there is to do. You will have to procrastinate on some things in your life. The key to personal achievement is to consciously select the things you're going to procrastinate on—the unimportant tasks—so you can concentrate on completing the tasks that will give you your highest payoff.

Five More Techniques

There are five more techniques that you can use to eliminate procrastination.

1. Slice the task. Just as you would never try to eat a whole loaf of salami at once, sometimes the best way to complete a major job is to take a small slice and complete it. You've heard the riddle: How do you eat an elephant? The answer is, of course, one bite at a time. There's a saying, "By the yard, it's hard, but inch by inch, anything's a cinch." Picking a small piece of the task, doing it, and getting it behind you is often a very effective way to help you get past procrastinating.

2. Start off your day by doing the task that causes you the most fear or anxiety. This usually has to do with someone else. It often has to do with overcoming the fear of failure or rejection. In sales, it may be associated with prospecting for leads; in management,

it may be associated with disciplining or firing an employee. In relationships, it may have to do with confronting an unhappy situation. In every case, you'll develop greater effectiveness if you discipline yourself to deal with the item that's causing you the greatest emotional distress first. After that, everything else during the day will seem relatively easier.

3. Similarly, you can overcome procrastination by starting the day with the most unpleasant task. A recent study compared two groups of people. One group started an exercise program and did their exercise routine in the morning. The second group started an exercise program and did it in the evening after work. The researchers found that the morning exercisers were much more likely to be in the program six months later. Starting the day with exercise was much more likely to lead to the habit of regular exercise than putting it off until the end of the day, when it was easier to make excuses and procrastinate.

4. Do away with perfectionism. Since perfectionism is a major reason for procrastination, decide not to worry about doing the job perfectly; just get started and work steadily. You can always go back and make corrections and revisions later. Nothing worthwhile has ever been done perfectly the first time anyway.

5. Maintain a fast tempo. A fast tempo is essential to success. Work at a brisk pace, walk quickly, move quickly, write fast, act quickly, get on with it. Maintain your momentum once you get it going. Remember the momentum theory, which says that it takes enormous effort to get into motion in the first place, but it takes much less effort to stay in motion. Consciously decide to speed up all your habitual actions. It's amazing how much you'll accomplish when you push yourself to move faster instead of staying at a normal slower pace.

The keys to getting things done are focus and concentration. Maximum performance requires that you:

- Clearly define your goals and objectives.
- Make action plans for their accomplishment.
- Make a list of everything that you have to do on a daily basis.
- Set clear priorities on the list.
- Concentrate single-mindedly on completing your most important tasks.

If you back up this method with a firm decision to work all the time you work, get back to work each time you're distracted, and develop a sense of urgency, you'll be able to produce two or three times the work of the average person, and you'll put your career into orbit.

An Action Exercise

Here's an action exercise. I assume by now that you have followed the previous recommendations: writing out your goals and objectives, making action plans for their accomplishment, and using a time planning system to ensure that every minute of every day is used effectively.

Now pick one area where procrastination is holding you back. Almost invariably, you'll be procrastinating on something that is potentially very important, something that can have major positive consequences for your future.

Pick this area, and decide to conquer procrastination here. Set priorities on your areas of procrastination, and then concentrate single-mindedly on this one area where overcoming your procrastination can make the greatest contribution to your success.

Attack the most difficult and unpleasant tasks first. Challenge yourself to confront the hardest parts of your work, and get them done before anything else. The rewards for getting control of your time, organizing yourself, and concentrating on completing your most important tasks can be enormous.

These time management habits go hand in hand with financial success and achievement. You'll also enjoy higher self-esteem, greater self-confidence, and greater pride in your ability to get things done. No other decision will be more satisfying and life-enhancing than the decision to set goals and objectives, set firm priorities, and do it now. Do it now.

Major Points

- The core of good time management is planning and organizing yourself for maximum productivity.
- Neatness counts.
- A good time management system makes use of time planners, calendars, and daily to-do lists.
- Understand the difference between the urgent and the important.
- Concentrate single-mindedly on the task with the highest payoff.
- Overcome procrastination by constantly telling yourself, "Do it now."

EIGHT

Streamline Your Life

In this chapter, I'm going to talk about streamlining your life and increasing your overall satisfaction and happiness by doing fewer things, and often by doing completely different things.

The Pipeline Model

The pipeline model of personal performance is one approach. If you can imagine a pipeline that stretches from point A to point B, you can see how it can be an analogy for your work life. Point A would be analogous to where you are now, and point B would be the equivalent of the goals that you want to accomplish. The way the pipeline is laid out, whether it's straight or crooked, whether it goes from point A to point B directly or indirectly, will have a lot to do with the quantity of material that flows through the pipeline, the speed at which it travels, and its level of production. That's why it's so important to be very clear about where you want to end up before you set off.

The productive capacity of the pipeline, which can be compared to your personal performance, is determined by two factors. The first is the size of the pipeline: the diameter. A large pipeline will carry more material than a smaller one.

In this analogy, the size of your pipeline is determined by your knowledge and skill: your productive capacity. The greater your level of knowledge and skill, the more productive you will be, and the more will flow through into your life. If you're a skilled sales-person or business executive, you have a highly developed ability to produce large quantities of high-value work. This capacity will be reflected in your lifestyle, your income, and your possibilities and opportunities for the future. If a person has limited skills, their pro-ductive capacity is quite small. No matter how clear their goals or how sincere their intentions, they won't be able to accomplish much.

So the first thing we know is that in order to improve the quality and quantity of the things that flow into your life, you must contin-ually work to improve and enlarge your productive capacity: your knowledge and skills.

The second factor that determines the rate of flow through the pipeline is the velocity of the material as it flows. If the commod-ity flowing through the pipeline is moving at five miles per hour, a certain amount will come out at the other end at a certain rate. However, if by the use of pumps, machinery, gravity, and other fac-tors, the velocity of material in the pipeline can be increased, far more can come through in the same time.

In your personal pipeline, your velocity is determined by both your effectiveness—what you do—and your efficiency: how well you do it. Time management increases the quality and quantity of your results by making you more effective and efficient. If you want more health, wealth, and happiness coming out of your pipeline of life, you need to think continually about increasing the size of the pipeline— your productive capacity—and the velocity of the flow through your pipeline: your effectiveness and efficiency. The quality and quantity of your life today is the direct result of the productive capacity and the velocity of your pipeline up to this moment. As you improve either or both, the quality of your life will improve simultaneously.

The Factory Model

The second model that helps you understand time is the factory model. If you've ever seen a large manufacturing plant, you've noticed that they're very long. An automobile plant, for example, can be a mile or more in length. In one end comes the raw materials, the raw steel, ready to be shaped, pressed, primed, painted, and drilled. As the raw materials move through the plant, they're assembled into engines, transmissions, rear ends, wheels, internal furnishings, and other parts. At the end of the process, out of the far end of the factory, comes the finished car.

Your life is similar to a factory in that raw material comes in one end and all of the aspects of your life come out of the other. The raw material is time. Every day you get another twenty-four hours: no more and no less than anyone else. In your factory of life, you process your time. Out of the other end come your home, your car, your bank account, your level of health and energy, your friends and relationships, and your present and future. When you stand back and look at what your factory of life is producing with the raw material of time, you may not be happy with some of what is coming out of the other end. If so, you need to go into your factory and change the production process. You need to intervene and do something different, sometimes very different, if you want to produce something better or different in your life. You've heard the old saying, "The more you do of what you're doing, the more you'll get of what you've got." Insanity has been defined as continuing to do the same things in the same way and expecting to get different results.

Time and Money

Time can also be compared to money. Time, like money, can be either spent or invested. If you spend it, it's gone forever. If you invest it wisely, it will earn you a return. A good investment of either time or money can earn you a high return over a sustained period of time. If a person saves their money and purchases a rental property, for example, it can give them an income for decades and can even be passed on to their children and grandchildren. On the other hand, if the person spends the money on an expensive vacation or an expensive car, the money is gone forever.

One additional parallel between time and money is that they're interchangeable up to a point. You can exchange time for money, and you can exchange money for time. For example, if you spend money to buy books or audio learning programs or take additional courses, you can increase your earning capacity: your ability to produce valuable results for which people will pay you. The money that you invest in learning can not only pay itself back many times over, it can save you months and even years of hard work to get to the same point in your financial life.

Little Zingers

I've spent many years and thousands of dollars studying time management. I've bought and read most of the time management books, listened to most of the audio programs, purchased most of the time planners on the market, and attended several time management seminars. Every so often, I come across ideas that have a powerful impact on my thinking about time and life. I call them paradigm shifters. These little zingers have changed my way of looking at time. I've already shared many of them with you, and now I want to share three more.

The first paradigm shifter for me was learning that every action or inaction involves a choice between what is more important and what is less important. Every time you do something, you're making a statement about where that activity ranks in your hierarchy of values. In fact, your entire life is a reflection of your choices up to now. A successful, happy person has made good choices, and a frustrated, unhappy person has made poor choices. Improving the quality of your choices inevitably leads to improving the quality of your life and your results. In everything you do, you're making a choice one way or the other.

The second paradigm shifter for me was discovering the law of the excluded alternative. This means that doing one thing means not doing something else. Every purchasing choice you make entails a rejection of all other choices. Similarly, every choice of activity involves a rejection of all other possible activities at that particular moment. When you choose to marry one person, you simultaneously reject everyone else in the world that you could marry.

You can only do or have one thing at a time. You can always tell (and so can others) what you consider most important by what you do, by the actions you take, by your choices at any given moment. A primary reason for success is that people choose deliberately to do things that enhance their lives more than other things. The reason for failure is that people choose to do things that do not enhance their lives, or even worse, make their lives and relationships worse than they would have been if they had done nothing at all.

Priorities and Posteriorities

The third paradigm shifter for me was learning that setting priorities means setting posteriorities as well. Each time you choose to do something, in order to do it properly, you must simultaneously decide what you are going to *stop* doing: your posteriority. To put it another way, taking hold means letting go. Getting in requires getting out; starting one thing means stopping something else.

Each time you choose to do something, you must decide what you are going to *stop* doing.

Most people feel overwhelmed with the pace of modern life. It's been estimated that you make more decisions in an average month than your grandparents made in a lifetime. If you live in the city, you're exposed to as many as 5,000 commercial messages per day. You have dozens of radio and television channels to choose from; you are inundated with correspondence and telephone calls. You're busy from dawn to dusk, and you probably don't feel that you're getting enough sleep. In one study, 62 percent of women reported that fatigue was their number one problem. When they got up in the morning, the first thing they thought about was what time they could go back to sleep that night.

Your dance card is full. You have *not* been bored for so long that you can't even remember. You're swamped with work and activities. You have places to go, people to see, things to do. You don't have a spare minute. You are probably living on the run. The point is this: if you agree to do something in addition to what you're already doing, you have no spare time available. You may have had spare time in the distant past, but you have none now.

Therefore, before you agree to do anything, you have to think about what you are going to stop doing in order to do something new. Most people continually add more time-consuming activities to their lives without thinking about the other activities that they're going to have to cut back on.

With mergers, acquisitions, downsizing, cutbacks, and the speed of technological change, people are being required to perform more and more functions at work. One of the best things that employees can do is to go to their boss with a list of everything that's on their plate and tell the boss that they can't do everything. If you're in this situation, tell your boss that you want to do the best job possible and ask him or her to set specific priorities on your tasks. What does your boss want you to do above all else? Make it clear that doing one thing means you won't be able to do other things on the list. There's only so much time in the day, and you cannot, even with the best time management techniques, do more than a certain amount.

Zero-Based Thinking

This brings us to one of the most important conceptual tools in modern life: *zero-based thinking*. Peter Drucker, perhaps the most admired management consultant of the twentieth century, emphasized the importance of this concept. Zero-based thinking means that you mentally draw a line under everything that you're doing and all the decisions that you've made in the past, and you ask yourself this key question: "Is there anything that I'm doing right now that, knowing what I now know, I wouldn't get into?"

This is an incredibly difficult question for most people. It requires tremendous courage to ask and answer this question of yourself. I can share this idea with an audience of a thousand people and ask them if there's anyone who is *not* in a situation that they wouldn't get into if they had to do it over. Of all these people, not one can raise their hand and say that there's nothing that they would change if they had to do it over.

It's not possible to manage your time to be more productive if, deep in your heart, you wouldn't even get into your current situation if you had to do it over again. There's no point in trying to be more effective in your work if you don't like the job or you're not suited for the position in the first place. There's no point in taking lessons on how to live more productively with a situation that you dislike. Worst of all is when you're in a relationship that, knowing what you now know, you wouldn't get into in the first place.

Ask yourself, knowing what you now know, is there any situation in your life that you wouldn't get into in the first place, if you had to do it over? If the answer is yes about any part of your life, your next question should be, "How do I get out of this situation? And how fast?"

Many people are spinning their wheels, with their lives on hold, trying to make a situation work that they'd rather be out of. However, all progress, all improvement, requires change, and change almost invariably means letting go of the old so that you can embrace the new. It means letting go of something of lower value so that you can embrace something of higher value.

Start by asking yourself with regard to your relationships, knowing what you now know, which of them would you choose not to get into in the first place? This takes tremendous courage, because many people are in relationships that they recognize are not working and are not likely to work, but they fear conflict and confrontation. If you're a manager, look at your staff and ask yourself, knowing what you now know, is there anyone that you would not hire if you had to do it over again? Almost every manager I've ever met has admitted that they have employees they would not choose if they had to do it over again.

Are there any investments that you're in or is there anything that you're purchasing that, knowing what you now know, you wouldn't get into in the first place? If so, what can you do to minimize your exposure? How can you get out of these investments? Are you involved in any activities that you don't particularly care about? Knowing what you now know, would you get into these activities again? If the answer is no, how do you get out, and how fast?

This is a terribly important part of time and life management. You can tell if there is something that you should not be in by looking at stress. A situation that is wrong for you will invariably cause you stress and anxiety. You will think about it too much of the time. You will talk about it at home. It'll be on the top of your mind and will come out in casual conversation. A wrong situation will drain emotional energy from you, sometimes at an incredible rate. Since you are responsible for maximizing your return on emotional energy, this is a lousy investment. Get out of it as soon as possible.

**A situation that is wrong for you will
invariably cause you stress and anxiety.**

Determining Value

Here's another paradigm shifter I've found. It's the discovery that the value of anything can be determined by how much of your time and your life you're willing to trade for it. The key word here is the word *trade*. Since you only have a certain number of hours and minutes in each day, with whatever you choose to do, you are trading part of your life for that activity. Because of the law of the excluded alternative, you are simultaneously taking that time away from other areas of your life. Everything you buy and everything you do is costing you a chunk of life that is gone forever and will never come back.

Look at yourself, your time, your life, and your activities in terms of how much of your precious time you're willing to trade, knowing that you will not have it to trade for something else. Your perspective on time, how you value it, and how you allocate it in both the short and the long term is a major determinant of everything that happens to you.

Political scientist Edward Banfield's work on success in America shows that success is largely attitudinal. It depends upon a person's time perspective. An individual with a long time perspective, one who takes the long view into consideration when making their day-to-day decisions, is far more likely to be economically successful than a person who ignores the long view. This usually entails making sacrifices in the short term so as to enjoy greater rewards in the long term.

Nevertheless, you must also develop a short time perspective. This means allocating your time in small amounts. The highest paid professionals in our society—doctors, lawyers, dentists, architects, engineers—allocate their time in blocks of one-tenth of an hour. If they charge $200 per hour for their services, they bill you for the number of six-minute blocks that they spend on your case. If they spend five minutes on a telephone conversation, you'll get a bill for one-tenth of an hour, so the bill will be for $20.

People at the top of their occupations or professions, salespeople, executives, or others who are earning high incomes, also have very tight time planning. They allocate their time in ten- and fifteen-minute chunks. They give a lot of thought to how their time will be spent. When they drive or travel, they use every minute productively.

Sadly, you can tell a person who's having financial troubles simply by asking them how their day is scheduled. People who aren't making much money have loose schedules. Research shows that the average blue-collar worker thinks in terms of two-week pay periods and seldom thinks more than two pay periods ahead. As one moves up the socioeconomic ladder, time horizons become narrower and narrower. People who are doing poorly in selling, for example, think in terms of the morning and the afternoon. People who are doing well in selling think in terms of fifteen-minute blocks, starting from 8:00 or 8:30 in the morning, and sometimes earlier, through to 6:00 in the evening and sometimes later. They may even have plans for additional work after they get home.

You can increase your income by beginning right now to plan your time as tightly as possible every single day, using some of the ideas that I've already discussed.

**You can increase your income by planning
your time as tightly as possible.**

Dinner versus Dessert

An endless amount of work has been done on success and failure, self-esteem and self-image, goals, personal productivity, and performance. The bottom line of all this work, however, has never really changed. If you could boil it down to a single phrase, it would be *self-discipline.* Successful, happy people have more self-discipline than unsuccessful, unhappy people. People who are moving up rapidly are more disciplined than people who are not. People who are accomplishing worthwhile things have a greater ability to discipline their time and their appetites than those who do not. Throughout history, the person with the greatest self-control and self-discipline has always dominated those with less.

In its simplest terms, self-discipline means the ability to have dinner before dessert. Much of life can be divided into dinner activities and dessert activities. You are surrounded by a thousand voices clamoring for your attention every single day, and almost every one of them is encouraging you to have dessert before or instead of dinner. Advertisements shout out at you to buy now, with no payments until January.

Dessert is served at a specific point in the meal: after the main course. It is not served first. If you eat dessert first, it kills your appetite for the main course. Moreover, dessert usually contains a lot of sugar and fat, so if you eat too much dessert rather than healthy main courses, it will eventually affect you physically, mentally, and emotionally. If you come home every night and eat chocolate cake and ice cream, you'll be overweight, you'll do less exercise, and you'll sit around and watch more television. The sugar will cause you to be more depressed, and you'll have less energy, less enthusiasm, and a crummier personality. By the same token, if you eat a rich, nourishing dinner full of healthy foods, your appetite for dessert will be greatly reduced. In many cases, you'll have no interest in dessert at all.

When you come home at night, dinner activities are things like talking to your spouse and playing with your children. Dessert activities are watching television, cracking a beer, and reading the newspaper. When you get home, you always have a choice between a dinner activity and a dessert activity. Which are you going to do first?

The great inspirational author Elbert Hubbard defined self-discipline as the ability to make yourself do what you should do when you should do it, whether you feel like it or not. The critical expression here is *feel like it or not.* Anybody can do something if they feel like it. When you don't feel like doing it, when it's hard, when you're tired and worn-out but you do it anyway because it's the right thing to do, you demonstrate character.

Character is what it's all about. One of the great aims of life is to develop character, to become a fine human being in the course of your personal evolution. The hallmark of the individual with character is self-discipline and self-restraint. The more you practice self-discipline, the better you feel about yourself, and the better a person you become. The less you practice self-discipline, the worse you feel about yourself, and the less admirable a person you become.

The hallmark of character is self-discipline and self-restraint.

In every case, ask yourself, is this a dinner activity or a dessert activity? Then deliberately choose to engage in the dinner activities until they're all done before you engage in the dessert activities. Out of this simple choice will issue all the results of your life.

Economics in One Lesson

Some years ago, Henry Hazlitt wrote a little book called *Economics in One Lesson*. Hazlitt was a writer for *The Wall Street Journal* and other publications for many years. He studied people, personalities, economics, and politics in great detail. Finally, he wrote his little book, which went on to sell more than a million copies. Many people who read it were forever changed in their attitudes and perspectives.

Hazlitt said that all wisdom is the accurate consideration of the secondary consequences of a particular act or decision. He said that the primary consequences are almost invariably positive: that's why a person engages in the activity in the first place. But the person has to live with the secondary consequences of the act, which are often re far worse than if nothing had been done at all.

Wisdom is the accurate consideration of the secondary consequences of a particular act or decision.

For example, the primary consequences of going out and having a couple of drinks after work are immediate enjoyment, socializing, personal gratification, relaxation, and a little fun. The secondary consequences are that for the rest of the evening, the person will be too befuddled to study something that will help them or even relate intelligently to others. The drinker will not be back to their normal self until the following day. The primary consequences are fun, but the secondary consequences are negative. It's the same when a person decides to exercise or not to exercise or to eat healthy foods or to eat sugary, fatty foods.

Secondary consequences kick in when a person decides to spend their evenings watching television instead of at the community college upgrading their skills and abilities. Secondary consequences kick in when a person spends much of their time bowling, socializing with friends, or doing work that they couldn't get done at the office because they've used their time poorly.

In every one of these cases, the primary consequences are usually fun and enjoyable, but the secondary consequences can be disastrous. In every situation, the wise person gives a lot of thought to the likely secondary consequences of the act.

The ability to consider secondary consequences is the hallmark of self-discipline and character. It is the true demonstration that the individual has developed a long time perspective. The accurate projection of secondary consequences and the selection of one's activities to assure that they are the very best possible is the prerequisite for success, happiness, and achievement.

It's like the game of chess. Before you make any decision, ask what is likely to happen as the result of this decision in the long term. What are the likely consequences? If they can be positive, it's probably a good thing to do. If the likely consequences can be negative, you must be very careful about your decision.

Today a person with a college degree earns 30 to 50 percent more per month than a person with only a high-school diploma. The extra two to four years of college pay themselves back in higher earnings in almost the same amount of time that it took to get the degree. From then on, the educated person will earn more and more as they progress through life. The uneducated person will be stuck in place, locked in a low-level job and doomed to continue at a low salary unless and until they upgrade their education.

The person who works hard in high school to get good grades and scrimps and saves to go on to college is concerned about the secondary consequences of their behavior. While all their friends are out partying and having a good time, this individual is plotting with a view to the long term. Before the dust settles, this person is living in a big house on the hill and driving a nice car, while the others are spinning their wheels.

There is a law of forced efficiency in personal management: although there's never enough time to do everything, there's always enough time to do the most important things. Your job is to think before acting and make sure you are doing the things that are most important rather than the things that are fun, easy, urgent, or convenient. Stand back from your life and continually ask, is this a good use of my time?

Although there's never enough time to do everything, there's always enough time to do the most important things.

The worst use of time is to do very well what need not be done at all. Many people become so busy doing unimportant things that they confuse activity with accomplishment. They don't stand back to look at their lives and realize that they're busy doing things that don't really matter; if they weren't done at all, it would make very little difference to their long-term success or failure. For example, a person could plan their workdays to have the longest and finest coffee breaks and lunch hours that one could ever want, and it would have almost zero impact on the important things that he or she wants to do with his or her life. Someone could read every sports page of every newspaper every day for the next twenty-five years, and it would have virtually zero impact on their life, career, and relationships.

The most important thing in time management is to choose. It is the highest demonstration of intelligence and wisdom. Your ability to make the right choices is the key to everything else. Your life is where it is and what it is as a direct result of the way you have used your time in the past. You can change your results and accomplishments by changing the way you use your time from this moment forward. You are always free to choose.

You can change your results by changing the way you use your time.

Work-Life Balance

People often ask how they can maintain balance between their work and their family. Everyone feels that they have too much to do in too little time. They feel that their relationships, especially their children, are suffering because of the incessant demands on their time from work, and they don't know what to do about it. They're concerned about holding on to their jobs, but they're equally concerned about maintaining the quality of their home lives.

The issue of balance is not going to go away. If anything, the speed of change and the demands of work will only intensify in the years ahead. It will continue to be a critical issue for the rest of your life, so any changes must be made in your heart, mind, and attitude.

Through a lifetime of study of philosophy, psychology, religion, and metaphysics, I've concluded that your level of happiness is the best indicator of whether your life is going well or not. At any time, you can look around and you'll find that best parts of your work and home are the parts where you feel the happiest and most at peace. Conversely, the areas where you feel unhappy, fearful, or anxious are your major problem areas and sources of stress.

Consequently, you should organize your life so that you have more and more parts where you are happy and fewer and fewer parts where you are unhappy.

This idea of using happiness as your barometer of what is right for you makes many people uncomfortable. They have been brought up being told that their own personal happiness is of secondary importance.

When I was growing up, I was told that the purpose of my life was to make others happy, and if I managed to seek out a little happiness on the way through, I should consider myself darn lucky. The idea of setting my own happiness as the centerpiece of my life was considered to be selfish, wrong, and unacceptable. But Abraham Lincoln wrote that you cannot help the poor by becoming one of them. By the same token, you cannot help people to be happy by being unhappy yourself. The idea that a person can suffer for the happiness of others is rather silly. You can't give away what you don't have. You can't make others happy unless you are a happy person yourself.

If you really love your spouse, work on yourself to become a positive and cheerful person, a joy and a delight to be around. If you really love your children, be a happy parent whom your children look forward to seeing every day.

Recent research suggests that children are much better off with a single parent who is happy than with two parents who are at each other's throats all the time. The old idea of staying together for the children is dead wrong. There's probably nothing more soul-destroying for a child than to live in a house full of animosity and bickering.

Nature is really wonderful in giving us everything we need to enjoy our lives. Nature builds mechanisms into us that let us know if something is good or bad for us, right or wrong. For example, if you touch something that is hot, you jerk your hand away immediately so that you don't burn yourself as an adult. You've had enough experiences with hot surfaces to know that they are dangerous. Nature gives you the sensation of physical pain to protect you from hurting yourself.

By the same token, nature has installed a guidance mechanism in you to tell you what is right and what is wrong for you in your personal, emotional, and business life. It is the sense of happiness versus unhappiness. All you have to do is to listen to yourself. When you're doing and saying what is right for you, you feel calm, comfortable, and happy inside. When you are doing, saying, or experiencing anything that is wrong for you, you feel nervous, angry, or fearful. In any situation, you can close your eyes and listen to your inner sense of happiness, and you'll always know the right thing for you to do.

A person who would never think of sitting on a hot stove and letting it burn them physically will stay in a situation where they are being emotionally burned for months and even years. Instead of listening to their feelings of unhappiness and accepting them as a guide, they ignore and suppress them and use psychological mechanisms to avoid dealing with the fact that they're miserable.

The most successful men and women are as a rule very clear about only doing things that makes them happy. They are equally adamant about refusing to get involved with people or situations that make them unhappy. If they get into such a situation, they deal with it directly and remove either the situation or themselves so they can get back to feeling at peace.

The most successful men and women are clear about only doing things that makes them happy.

Many people stay in unhappy situations because they think that somehow they're going to gain something that will more than compensate for the misery. This seldom happens. When you think back through your life to the times that you have spent unhappily, whether in a bad relationship, a bad job, or a bad business situation, you will probably recall that you never got anything worthwhile.

In retrospect, you would never have gotten into it, and once in, you would have gotten out a lot sooner.

Nothing good comes of something bad. Superior people have learned from long experience that it doesn't pay anyway. Individuals who refuse to subject themselves to any situation that makes them feel unhappy for any period of time. They will either change the situation or walk away. They will pay whatever price it takes, but they will not sacrifice their happiness or their emotional integrity for someone or something else.

Once you've decided to use your own happiness as the guide to your decisions, you will undoubtedly realize that fully 85 percent of your happiness comes from your relationships with others. Of course, fully 85 percent of your unhappiness comes from your relationships with others as well. Most of our joys come from people, and most of our sorrows come from them as well. If you're really concerned about your happiness, you must be concerned about the way you interact with others. People are not peripheral to a good life; they are the very heart and essence of a good and happy life.

Design Your Ideal Life

To get your life in balance and keep it there, it is essential to reflect and think about who you are, where you're going, and what you really care about. Just as we saw with strategic thinking, you begin with your values. You ask yourself continually, "What is really important to me? What do I really care about? Why am I doing what I'm doing?"

People frequently get out of balance because they stop thinking, and they mask this fact with frantic activity. They get busier and busier and more tired, doing more and more things of lesser and lesser value. They feel like a rat on a treadmill, going faster and faster and not getting anywhere. They don't know how to stop because they've lost sight of the fact that their ability to think is the most powerful tool they have to ensure a happy, healthy life. Some people have to have massive heart attacks to slow them down and get them to think. Others have to have life-threatening illnesses. Some have to have their marriages collapse. We humans are funny in that often we need a good slap in the face to get our attention.

Once you've decided on your values, take some time with a pad and paper to describe your ideal lifestyle. If you could design the perfect life from dawn to dusk, from Monday to Friday, from the beginning of the year to the end, how would you like to live? Sit with your spouse and design your dream life. Where would you like to live? What would you like to be doing? How many hours a day would you like to be doing it? What would you like to be doing in your leisure time? If your company or industry collapsed completely and left you out on the street, free to make any choice at all about your future occupation, what would you want to do? Whom would you want to do it with? How much would you like to be earning?

Go through your list of different goals. Decide your ideal level of health and fitness, your ideal weight, the subjects you'd want to learn more about, the activities you'd like to engage in, the people you'd like to socialize with, and especially the way you'd like to spend time with the people who are closest to you.

Once you've worked out a definition of your ideal lifestyle, take a look at where you are now. Imagine that you have a pad of paper and draw a ball the left side of the paper and another ball on the right side of the paper. In the first ball, write, "Now," and in the second, write "Five years." Then ask yourself, "What would I have to do, starting today, to begin moving from where I am now to where I want to be in five years in each area of my life?"

The best way to predict your future is to create it. The best way to ensure that you are where you want to be in five years is to design it as you would design a house. Then begin building your life step by step and day by day, so that five years from now you arrive at your preplanned destination.

To achieve balance in your life, set peace of mind as your highest goal, and organize your time and your life around it. Your inner voice, your intuition, is your inner guide to peace and contentment, and it will never lead you astray. When you set peace of mind as your umbrella goal and you organize all of your other goals and activities of your life under it, you are much less likely to make major mistakes.

An Action Exercise

Imagine that you had only one hour left to live. What would come into your mind? What would you think about? What would you do in your last sixty minutes? My guess is that a face or faces would come into your mind; you would think about the person or persons that you would want to reach out and touch.

I don't know whose face or faces came into your mind. I only know one thing for sure: if you had only sixty minutes left to live, you would not be thinking, "I'd like to get back to the office and return a few phone calls." The whole purpose of personal time management is to enable you to fulfill your responsibilities to the outside world so that you have more time to spend with the most important people in your life, with the persons whose faces would come into your mind if you learned that you only had a short time to live. The aim of time management is to allow you to spend more time with the people you love, doing more of the things you really enjoy, and the time to begin is now.

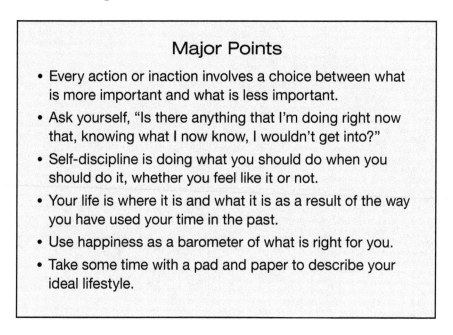

Major Points

- Every action or inaction involves a choice between what is more important and what is less important.
- Ask yourself, "Is there anything that I'm doing right now that, knowing what I now know, I wouldn't get into?"
- Self-discipline is doing what you should do when you should do it, whether you feel like it or not.
- Your life is where it is and what it is as a result of the way you have used your time in the past.
- Use happiness as a barometer of what is right for you.
- Take some time with a pad and paper to describe your ideal lifestyle.

NINE

Increase Your Earning Ability

To fulfill your potential, you must develop a lifelong commitment to enhancing your earning ability. No matter who signs your paycheck, you are always self-employed; you are the president of your own personal services corporation. You are 100 percent responsible for your own research and development, that is, constantly working on yourself to increase the value of your contribution. Your ability to get valuable results will, more than any other factor, determine how much you earn. Lifelong learning is now a minimum requirement for success in any field. It's the springboard to higher earnings and job security. It's the antidote to job loss in a rapidly shifting economy.

Why, then, don't people don't engage in personal and professional development? The major reason is a lack of goals and plans. A person who has no clear sense of direction sees no pressing reason to learn anything new. A lack of goals leads to a lack of commitment, especially to oneself and one's future.

I've already pointed out that you can measure the importance of anything you do by assessing its potential impact on your future. If something has a major potential impact on your future, it's important to do in the present. If something has a low potential impact on your future, it's not particularly important to do in the present, or perhaps ever. Long time perspective, which guarantees future success, requires doing things in the short term that will have a major impact in the long term.

One of the most valuable activities is to learn, develop your mind, and invest in increasing your earning ability. When you read a book, listen to an audio recording, or attend a seminar, you may learn something useful that affects your career for decades. It can even have a positive future impact on yourself, your family, your children, and your children's children. When you increase your income and move into a higher socioeconomic group, you are giving your children opportunities to move up into the same group as well. A generation from now, your children's children can still benefit as a result of your present investment in yourself.

What Do You Need to Know?

I've become a strong believer in the power of personal and professional development. I believe that you can become anything that you want if you can clearly identify what you want and study to learn what you need to know.

I've said that you must ask, what additional knowledge or information will you need in order to achieve your goal? If your goal is to become financially independent, you have to become very good at what you do. What do you need to learn to be the best in your field? Only when you commit yourself to going any distance, making any sacrifice, and spending any amount of time necessary to learn what you need to be the best can you be sure that you will achieve your goals.

Your ability to get valuable results for which someone else can pay you can be compared to water in a bucket. When you start your career, the results you can get are at a minimum. You have limited knowledge and experience; therefore the amount you can earn is also limited. Your bucket of earning capacity has very little in it. As time passes, you pour more knowledge and experience into the bucket. As your knowledge increases, the level rises, and your level of income rises as well. If you keep putting more knowledge and experience into the bucket, your results will eventually rise to the point where your level of income will be higher as well.

However, there's a small problem with this bucket: it has a hole in it. This means that every day, some of your knowledge and experience is draining out, becoming obsolete or useless. Your earning ability will diminish over time if you do nothing to continually increase it as you go along. To counteract this loss, you must continually put more knowledge into the top of the bucket than is dripping out of the bottom. The person who stops learning doesn't stay in place: they begin to slide backward as their earning capacity begins to leak away.

Successful people are not necessarily smarter than unsuccessful people; they simply know more of the important things. They have paid the price to move ahead by learning more about what they're doing. Sometimes one small bit of extra knowledge can change the whole direction of your career and enable you to make a giant leap forward.

Every improvement begins with taking in new information: gaining a new insight or understanding of ourselves or our work. Successful men and women continually bombard their minds with new ideas from a variety of sources. They wade into the river of knowledge and open themselves up to a continuous stream of information.

To earn more, you must learn more. You cannot earn any more than you're earning today except to the degree to which you learn and practice something new. You are plateaued at this moment. You have reached your maximum income at your current level of knowledge. Every bit of progress that you make from this moment forward will depend upon learning something new or different and acting on it.

To earn more, you must learn more.

Applying the Mental Laws

I've discussed the law of correspondence, which says that your outer world is a reflection of your inner world. Your outer world of wealth and accomplishments tends to correspond to your inner world of learning and preparation. For this reason, you seldom learn anything new and valuable without soon getting an opportunity to put it into practice.

This brings us again to the law of attraction, which says that everything you have, you have attracted into your life by the person you are. You can attract more because you can change the person you are. The law of attraction is so powerful that if you commit yourself to upgrading your skills, you'll almost immediately begin attracting into your life people, circumstances, ideas, and even job offers to enable you to use your new knowledge. You'll set up a force field of energy that attracts what other people call luck, but which you will know is the direct result of your own work on yourself.

Another important law is the law of cause and effect, with its sublaw, the law of sowing and reaping. The law of cause and effect says that for every effect in your life, real or desired, there is a spe-

cific cause. The cause of wealth, success, and high achievement is
hard work, commitment, and unending preparation. The law of
sowing and reaping says that whatever you are reaping today is the
result of what you have sown in the past, especially in your mind.
To reap something different in the future, sow something different
in the present. Once you've sown the seeds of new knowledge, the
reaping—the opportunity to use that knowledge—will appear.

Perhaps the most important laws regarding personal and professional development is the law of accumulation, which says that
every great accomplishment is an accumulation of hundreds, even
thousands, of hours and efforts that no one else sees or appreciates. It is summed up beautifully in a poem by Henry Wadsworth
Longfellow:

> *The heights by great men reached and kept*
> *Were not attained by sudden flight,*
> *But they, while their companions slept,*
> *Were toiling upward in the night.*

The law of accumulation says that everything counts. Everything you're doing or not doing on a daily basis counts. Everything
is being written down in a big book and is either going on the credit
side or the debit side of the ledger. Everything that you're doing is
either moving you toward your goals or away. Every hour that you
read, every hour that you listen to audio recordings, every hour that
you spend in seminars and lectures counts. Every hour is adding up
to either a great life or a mediocre life, and the clock is running.

Now for some advice that will change your life forever: from this
day forward, invest 3 percent of your annual income back into your
own personal and professional development. As Benjamin Franklin

said, "Empty the coins of your purse into your mind and your mind will fill your purse with coins." If you invest this amount of your income back into yourself, in a very short time you will find that you will never have to worry about money again. (The converse is also true: if you do *not* invest part of your income in yourself, you will probably have to worry about money for the rest of your life.) If you follow this advice, you'll reach the point where you do not have enough days and weeks in the year to spend all of the extra money. If you begin right now to invest 3 percent of your income into your mind, you will be astonished at how rapidly your whole life begins to transform.

Three Areas of Development

There are three primary areas of personal and professional development. The first is to read everything that you can get your hands on that will help you.

Unfortunately, many people have come out of school unable to read. They find reading difficult and avoid it whenever possible. They are accustomed to taking in their information through television, radio, and the Internet—that is, passively rather than through the active medium of the written word.

If you're a poor reader, there are countless ways you can learn to read. Many companies have remedial reading programs, as do YMCAs, community colleges, high schools, and universities. There's a large and growing national literacy program, which actively searches for students to match with trained tutors. If you want to learn to read well, there's nothing in the world to stop you.

All leaders are readers, and only reading is reading; there's no substitute for it. Reading is to the mind as exercise is to the body.

Nothing more fully engages your entire brain in the act of learning than concentrating on the written word. Many people make excuses for not reading, but these are only exercises in self-delusion. If you have a reading problem, set a goal this very minute to become excellent at reading a year or two from today. Your reading problems will be a thing of the past, and you'll be rewarded in more ways than you can imagine.

How much should you read? If you read one hour per day in your field and take good notes, within three years, you'll be an authority in any field you choose. Within five years, you'll be a national expert. Within seven years, you'll be an international expert.

Reading one hour per day will translate into roughly one book per week. One book per week will translate into approximately fifty books per year. Fifty books per year will translate into approximately 500 books over the next ten years. The average American reads less than one nonfiction book per year; 58 percent of Americans never read another nonfiction book after they leave high school. As a result, if you were to read just one book per month that helped you to grow personally or professionally, it would put you into the top 1 percent of adult learners in America. If you invest one hour per day reading in your field, you'll be putting your foot on the accelerator of your own potential. Because of the law of correspondence, your outer life will begin to change dramatically.

Audio and Video Learning

The second place where you can invest your income back into your mind is in audio and video learning. The finest minds alive today have summarized their best thoughts on professionally produced audios. In fact, the invention of audio learning is probably the greatest breakthrough in education since the invention of the printing press. I've met and spoken to thousands of men and women whose lives have been profoundly changed by listening to audios. Unfortunately, most people have never listened to an educational audio in their lives. For some reason, they think that it's not for them—that audios are too expensive or wouldn't help them.

According to the American Automobile Association, the average car owner in America drives between 12,000 and 25,000 miles per year. Taking traffic into consideration, this translates into something between 500 and 1,000 hours that you spend sitting in your car every year. This is the equivalent of twelve and a half to twenty-five paid weeks per annum. Imagine what it would mean if your boss gave you twelve and a half to twenty-five paid weeks—three to sixth months—every year for ongoing education. Do you think that would affect your income? You bet it would. This amount of time translates into one to two university semesters. You can become one of the best-educated and best-paid individuals of your generation simply by listening to audios as you drive around. Turn your car into a university on wheels, and turn driving time into learning time.

Seminars and Workshops

The third place to invest your 3 percent is in seminars, workshops, and ongoing courses of study. Only take courses from experts: men and women who have achieved success in their fields and are now teaching others how to do the same thing.

When you go to workshops and seminars, sit as close to the front as you can, and take copious notes. Take every opportunity to follow up the sessions by asking questions and getting insights and advice.

Sometimes you can ask a question and get a piece of information that will be worth thousands of dollars and save you months of hard work.

At these seminars, take every opportunity to meet the other participants. Hand out your business cards and get theirs. Use this opportunity to build up your network. The type of people who go to seminars and workshops are ambitious, hardworking, eager to learn, and willing to invest in themselves. These are the kind of people that you want to get to know.

Beginning Your Quest

Where do you begin your lifelong quest for knowledge? Start right where you are. Look at your current job and ask, "What knowledge or skills would it be useful for me to have if I wanted to move ahead?"

**Ask, "What knowledge or skills would it be useful
for me to have if I wanted to move ahead?"**

Begin with the most relevant and useful knowledge that you can apply right now. Don't worry about learning things that you may need a year or five years from now. This just leads to distraction and dispersion of your efforts. Be focused and selfish about what you choose to learn in the short term. Learn only what you can use immediately to get better results.

Earl Nightingale said that you will always be paid in direct proportion to what you do, how well you do it, and the difficulty of replacing you. You must always be thinking in terms of what you are doing and what you want to do in the future. What will you have to learn in order to be prepared to do what you want to do two, three, or five years from now?

You will always be paid in direct proportion to what you do, how well you do it, and the difficulty of replacing you.

Once you've chosen your field, concentrate on becoming supremely good at it. Furthermore, you must make every effort to make yourself indispensable. If you can do this, your future is largely assured. You'll never have to worry about a job, and you'll never have to worry about money for long.

We live in a knowledge-based society. Fully 70 percent of all men and women working in America today are involved in some phase of generating, processing, and distributing information, and the percentage of knowledge-based workers is increasing every year. You have no choice but to incorporate yourself into the knowledge and information economy by becoming extremely knowledgeable about your chosen field. Read *Success, Inc., Forbes, Fortune, Business Week,* and any specialized publications that deal with your profession.

Purchase books by successful people in your field. Build up your own library. When you read these books, make notes and underline so that you can come back to the important parts and find them easily later.

The OPIR Method

You can do some important things to enhance your ability to learn. Studies conducted on superlearning have concluded that listening to classical music in the background while you read and study accelerates learning speed and information retention.

Another good idea is to have a quiet place where you go to study on a regular basis. By doing this, you train your mind to be ready to absorb information when you sit down and begin.

To get the most out of a book, use the four-step **OPIR** method:

O: Before you begin a book, do an *overview*. Read the front and back. Read the table of contents, and flip through the book to see how it's laid out.

P is for *preview*. Read through the book one page at a time, turning the pages as rapidly as you can and getting a feel for the chapter headings and the subheads, which give the major ideas.

I stands for *in-view*. This is how you read in depth. A good recommendation is to read the book in the order of your own personal interests. You don't necessarily follow the order that the author has laid out (except in a fiction book); instead go straight to the chapters that interest you the most, from there to the chapters that interest you the second most, and so on. You may find that there's only one chapter that's of interest to you at this moment. In that case, read only that chapter and then put the book away for another time.

R stands for *review*. Since you forget fully 50 percent of what you learned within two hours, if you quickly review a book immediately after having read everything in it that you consider valuable, you will double or triple your retention level.

It's also useful to underline with a red pen or use a highlighter on critical sentences and ideas. With this method, it may take me five or six hours to read a book the first time, but then I can reread all the key ideas in less than an hour.

Some books are only meant to be scanned quickly. Some should be read completely from one end to the other, but not read again. Others are full of information that's extremely relevant to what you're doing, and these books can be reread again and again, enabling you to reach new depths of understanding at each reading.

Just as you make eating, sleeping, exercising, and socializing a regular part of your daily life, make reading, learning, and studying a regular part of your activities. Have a specific place in your home where you study, and set a regular study schedule.

You can tell with considerable accuracy where you're going to be and what you're going to be doing in three to five years by the amount of time you spend in investing in your mind. My friend Charlie Jones says that in five years, you will be where you are today except for the books you read and the people you meet.

Your commitment to ongoing personal and professional development is perhaps the most important single thing that you can do in your career. It will open doors and make you capable of taking advantage of many opportunities, and it's totally under your own control. A commitment to ongoing personal development is an outward expression of self-discipline, self-mastery, and long-term perspective. It's a mark of personal character in all superior men and women.

The 1,000 Percent Formula

Let me now explain my 1,000 percent formula. It is based on the proposition that it is possible for you to increase your income by 1,000 percent or 10 times over the next 10 years. It's based on the law of accumulation, and it's very simple. I've used this method to increase my own income by 100 times over a period of 12 years. Many of my students have used it to increase their income by even more.

The first question I have to ask is simply this: is it possible for you—if you really wanted to, if you really concentrated—to increase your productivity, performance, and output by 0.5 percent over the next 7 days? If you think about this question, you will realize that just by applying a little bit of what you already know about time management, you could easily be 0.5 percent more effective over the next 7 days.

Can you increase your productivity by 0.5 percent over the next 7 days?

Now, having improved your effectiveness for 7 days, could you do it for the next 7 days? Of course you could. If you could do it for one 7-day period, you could do it for another 7-day period. Could you do it every week for a month? Your answer again would have to be yes.

By the end of the third week, you would have triggered the momentum principle of personal development: you would find yourself moving and growing more rapidly each week as long as you persisted in improving your effectiveness a little every single day.

Having increased your productivity for the first month, could you do it for the second month, and the third? Could you do it for an entire year? Again, your answer will be yes. If you really wanted to, you could maintain this momentum indefinitely. In fact, the longer you increase your personal effectiveness, the easier it will become. Having done it for the first year, could you do it for the second year, the third, and the fourth? Of course.

Here's how the numbers work out: If you improve your effectiveness by 0.5 percent each week, that would equal a 2 percent increase in your productivity over the course of 4 weeks. A 2 percent increase in your productivity each 4 weeks, over the course of 13 4-week periods—52 weeks—would be a total of 26 percent improvement in one year. Furthermore, everything you do to increase your effectiveness in any area has an impact on every other area. So your effectiveness would compound over the 52 weeks, 26 percent each year. Multiply this figure by 10 years, and with compounding, it would equal 1,004 percent at the end of the 10th year.

In short, you could increase your total productivity performance and output by 1,004 percent over 10 years by simply using the law of accumulation and improving at the rate of 0.5 percent per week. If you have the self-discipline to maintain this rate of improvement, I can assure you that you will get these results and perhaps even greater results.

Seven Parts of the Formula

Almost everyone who has tried the methodology I'm about to give you has told me that 26 percent per year is too low. They have experienced 50 percent, 100 percent, and even 300 and 400 percent increases in productivity, performance, and income in as little as 6 months. Here are the seven parts of the 1,000 percent formula.

1. Arise early each morning and read educational, motivational, or inspirational material for 30 to 60 minutes. If you invest 30 to 60 minutes in your mind each morning, your entire day will be better. You'll feel happier and more positive. You'll be more productive. If all you did was to read 30 to 60 minutes each morning and nothing else, that alone would probably give you your 1,000 percent increase over the next 10 years, if not before.

2. Write and rewrite your major goals in the present tense every morning. Use a spiral notebook and spend 3 to 5 minutes writing out your goals. This programs them deeper and deeper into

your subconscious mind and makes you more alert and aware all day of opportunities to achieve them.

3. Plan every day in advance. Write out a blueprint for every day before you begin, and follow the blueprint every hour of the day.

4. Set priorities, and always concentrate on the most valuable use of your time. If all you did was to set careful priorities based on your most important goals and objectives and concentrate only on the most valuable use of your time, that alone would probably give you your 1,000 percent increase.

5. Listen to educational audios in your car. Never allow your automobile to be moving without an educational audio. Remember, everything counts. Every minute that you spend learning is moving you that much closer toward the fulfillment of your goal of financial independence.

6. Ask two questions. After every situation, every interview, every sales call, and every difficulty, ask, "What did I do right?" and "What would I do differently?" These questions will enable you to learn at an accelerated rate.

7. Treat everyone you meet like a million-dollar customer. Treat everyone you meet, starting with your family at home in the morning, as well as people throughout the day, as though he or she were the most important person in the world. Everyone already considers himself or herself to be the most important person in the world. If you recognize this, it will do more to smooth your path in human relationships than any other single attitude.

The key to your future is ongoing, continual, persistent, personal and professional development. There is nothing that you cannot be. There is nothing that you cannot achieve. There is nowhere that you cannot go and nothing that you cannot become if you are willing to invest your time and money back into your mind and keeping at it long enough and hard enough to achieve your goals.

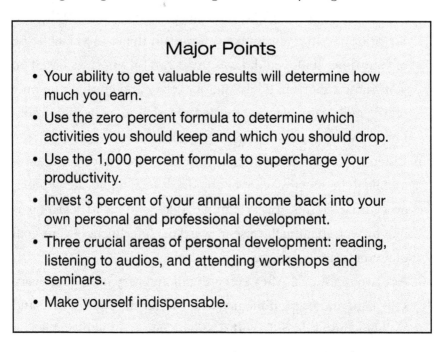

Major Points

- Your ability to get valuable results will determine how much you earn.
- Use the zero percent formula to determine which activities you should keep and which you should drop.
- Use the 1,000 percent formula to supercharge your productivity.
- Invest 3 percent of your annual income back into your own personal and professional development.
- Three crucial areas of personal development: reading, listening to audios, and attending workshops and seminars.
- Make yourself indispensable.

TEN

Get the Job You Want

One great secret of success is to do what you love. You'll be more successful doing what you enjoy than at any other job you could elect. In fact, one of the best ways to waste your life and to eliminate any possibility of happiness in your career is to work at something that you don't like just for the money or the security.

Fully 80 percent of men and women working today are underemployed: their jobs don't fully utilize all of their talents and abilities. Perhaps less than 5 percent of employed people in America feel that they are working at their full potential. Your primary career responsibility is to adamantly refuse to work at anything you don't enjoy. To do this, you must take 100 percent responsibility for getting and keeping the job you want.

The average person begins a career by taking whatever job is offered when they leave school. This often begins a lifelong habit of allowing other people to control their career path. The individual stays at the job until they are either promoted, demoted, or fired. Then they look for someone else to give them a place to work. They remain totally at the mercy of whoever decides to offer them a job and a paycheck.

The Creative Job Search

In this chapter, you're going to learn how to join the creative minority who move into and up in the jobs they want. One of the fastest ways to get an increase in pay is to move to a job that pays more. The best combination is to do something you enjoy that offers both higher pay and greater opportunities for advancement.

Fortunately, thousands of jobs are available for you. You are surrounded by a vast job market that, like an ocean, is largely invisible but nonetheless exists. If you can decide exactly what you want, you can use a variety of goal setting and goal achieving techniques to get it. This especially applies to creative job searching. If you can decide exactly what kind of job you want, you'll learn how to get it in the shortest time possible.

You are surrounded by a vast job market.

Creative job search begins with you. Sit down with a pad and pen and describe your ideal job. When you think about your ideal job, you should think about several things:

1. What would you most enjoy doing?
2. What have you been good at in the past?
3. What are you best qualified to do?
4. What have you done in your career that has been most successful for you and your company?

Begin your job search with a rigorous self-assessment. Look into yourself and decide who you are, what you can do, and most of all, what you would ideally like to do in the future. You may take psychological tests to get a better handle on your personality and interests. You may ask other people, including those close to you, what they think would be the best thing for you to be doing. Often people who are close to you can see possibilities for you that you are not aware of yourself. Ask, what are your unique talents and strengths? What do you do very well? Where do you excel? What sort of work really interests you? If you won a million dollars in the lottery and you could work at anything you wanted to for the rest of your life, what job would you choose?

When you describe your ideal job, write out the kind of work that you would like to do day in and day out. What kind of income would you ideally like to earn? What kind of people would you like to work with? What kind of values would you want the company you work for to have? Where would you like your work to be located? Since your skills are portable, you can work anywhere in the country you want. You can move from the Northeast to the Southwest, from the Northwest to the Southeast. You can work in any kind of climate, in any part of the nation where you enjoy the environment and lifestyle. There are no limitations except the ones you place on your own mind and imagination.

What size company would you like to work for? A large company or a small company? What kind of corporate culture would you be most comfortable with? Would you prefer to work for a traditional company, with a hierarchical structure, or would you prefer to work for a more nontraditional or relaxed company, with a flattened management structure? And of course, what kind of industry would you like to work in?

If you're currently working for someone else or you're unemployed, this process will help you get a better job faster than any other. I've taught this material to thousands of men and women, and my students have a 90 percent success rate at getting the job they want within six weeks.

Creative job search begins with taking full responsibility for the rest of your career and not leaving it up to any employer to decide what you'll do and where you'll do it. Creative job search requires looking into yourself and doing regular self-examinations so that you know exactly what you want to do, where you want to do it, and whom you want to do it with.

Where to Find the Job You Want

There are millions of job markets. Every company, every department in every company, and every decision-maker who has hiring authority is a job market. In recent years, online resources such as LinkedIn have also become important. To get the job you want, you only have to find and impress one person with the idea that you can give him or her greater value for which he or she is willing to pay, and you can create a job for yourself.

Over 85 percent of all available jobs are never advertised or published. If you read every newspaper and apply to every ad and send out résumés to every name and address you can get, you'll only be making yourself known to about 15 percent of the entire job market. The worst thing about answering traditional job search ads and sending out résumés is that it is terribly competitive and extremely frustrating. One study concluded that it took an average of 1,470 résumés mailed out to generate one job offer. Those are odds you cannot afford to play around with. Life is just too short. Furthermore, 85 percent of jobs in the invisible job market are invariably filled as the result of contacts. That is, either someone you know has a friend or associate who needs someone with your talent and ability, or you make the contacts yourself, either directly or indirectly. Direct ways of making contacts will be described later in this chapter, as will indirect methods of making and networking.

Many jobs are created when the right person comes along. Most companies realize that their growth is only limited by the number of talented people they can attract and keep. Successful and progressive companies are always on the lookout for talented individuals who can help them expand the quality and quantity of the products and services that they sell.

Many companies are hiring at the same time that they're laying people off. It's generally accepted in America today that if a good person walks in the door, you grab that person, hold on to them, and you figure out what you're going to do with that person later. Your job is to be perceived by the employer as the kind of person that they should hire on the spot, pay good money to, and give ample opportunity for advancement.

The more specific you are about the type of job you want, the easier you are to hire and the less competition you'll face. The more research that you do before you sit down with an employer, the more able you'll be to present yourself as the ideal person for a position.

The more specific you are about the type of job you want, the easier you are to hire.

When you have a clear idea of your ideal job but you've never done it before, do research on the business, the industry, and even on the city or state where you want to work. Begin with the most general. Do extensive online research through Google and similar search engines. Go down to the local library and look through the encyclopedias. Gather all the information in note form that you can about the kind of work, the industry, and the part of the country you want to work in. Once you have a general understanding of the field, you can read trade magazines, articles, and stories on the industry, both online and in print. You can go down to the library and read or check out books such as *The 100 Best Companies to Work For in America*. Read in your chosen field until you have questions, and then talk to people and ask questions until you need to read again.

If you're interested in a particular field, seek out people in the field and ask them about it. Most people who are working in a particular profession love to talk about what they're doing. Through your own efforts or through contacts, get hold of someone, take them out to lunch, and ask every question you can about the business or industry that you're interested in. Use your contacts; tell members of your family that you're interested in getting more information about this company or industry. Tell your friends that you're thinking of making a career change into this industry, and ask them if they know anybody or have any information on it. In casual conversations, mention that you're in the midst of a job search. You'll be amazed at how many people have information for speeding up the process of getting the job you want.

Above all, be sure to ask for referrals and recommendations from everyone. Remember, there's a direct relationship between the number of people you know and your likely success in getting your ideal job.

Ask for referrals and recommendations from everyone.

Informational Interviewing

This brings us to the core skill of creative job search: informational interviewing. This is the process by which you select the companies you might like to work for. The top 5 percent of job seekers in America use informational interviewing. It will get you more and better information, more and better job offers, and more and better opportunities to move up rapidly. Everyone who uses it is astonished by how quickly they get results.

Informational interviewing is based on the premise that your life is valuable. You're not about to go out and just go to work for anyone who offers you a job. You are going to carefully select the place where you want to work and determine whether or not a given company offers you the human environment and culture that you are looking for. Ask a lot of questions, and keep your options open. All of these requirements are fulfilled by informational interviewing.

Let's say you have decided to get a job in a particular industry. You will have gone to the library, done online research, and read everything you could find on that industry. You'll have spoken to friends, and you'll have read all the publications you could find on that industry. As your search continues, you'll become aware of the leading companies in that industry in the city where you've decided you want to live. Your next step is to begin contacting these companies and asking for ten or twenty minutes of the time of an executive who is in a likely position to hire for the job you're looking for.

When you get to the interview, explain that you are doing some research in this field because you're thinking of making a career change, and you would like to ask the executive a few questions to help you decide.

Here's an example of how this process works: Some years ago, I decided that I wanted to be a copywriter. At the time, I wasn't even sure what a copywriter was, but I had an idea that it was a job writing and creating advertising for various products. First I visited an advertising agency and spoke to the copy chief. I explained to him that I was interested in the field. He asked me a few questions and told me that my qualifications were not such that anyone would hire me at the present time. I asked him for his advice, and he suggested that I learn more about what was involved in copywriting and how to do it. At the time, I was working for a large department store chain. However, I was dissatisfied and frustrated because I wasn't earning very much money and I didn't enjoy the work. So I went down to the public library and checked out books on copywriting. I read books on the development of the profession as well as on how to write copy effectively. Over the next year, I wrote sample copy for advertisements and took it to various advertising agencies in the city. I started with the smaller agencies, taking my material to them, showing them what I had done, and asking for their advice on how to go further. During the next six months, I applied for jobs at almost every advertising agency in the city. After every interview, I would ask the person who had turned me down what I would have to do to improve. I learned enough that at the end of six months, I was accepted as a junior copywriter by the largest advertising agency in the city. When I look back at the process, I realize that I stumbled into this creative job search methodology without even knowing it. You too can make this methodology work.

Here are some questions that you might ask during an informational interview:

How long has the company been in business?

How long has it been in this city or in this state?

What is the major product or service sold by this company?

What type of people or organization uses your products or services the most?

What influence is the current economy having on your business?

How do you see the business developing over the next year? How about the next three to five years?

What sort of skills are in greatest demand in this business?

Where do you see the opportunities opening up for people in this business in the near future?

Finally, if you could resolve one problem or difficulty facing you in this business, what would it be?

You could go on to ask some personal questions of the person you're interviewing. For example, you could ask, how long have you been in this business or how long have you been in this position? You could ask, what did you do before this? Why did you change? How did you get into this business anyway? How do you like this field? Would you recommend it to others? What advice could you give to a person who is interested in a career in this field? And finally, can you suggest anything that I could read that would help me better understand this business?

Asking each of these questions gives you an opportunity to listen to the answer. Be sure to write down your answers on a pad of paper in full view of the person you are talking to. Sometimes people who are searching for jobs will interview prospective employers as though they were planning to write an article on the subject of the interview. Keep very good notes so that the employer will see that you are serious. Employers are impressed with people who ask intelligent questions and listen carefully to the answers. Listening builds trust.

This informational interview helps you get a feel for the employer while enabling the employer to get a feel for you. Neither of you has to make any decision. Keep your informational interview to twenty minutes or less. When the time is up, thank the employer for his or her time and prepare to depart. Be polite, be friendly, and be grateful for the time. Immediately after the interview, send a thank-you note or email.

Call Them Back

Once you found someone you would like to work for in a company where you would like to work, call the individual back and tell him or her that you would like to get together for a few minutes to explain your findings. Almost invariably, if you've been a pleasant interviewer and have impressed the employer favorably, you'll be invited back for a follow-up meeting very soon. When you sit down with a decision-maker, explain your findings and explain your research process, which has led you to conclude that you want to work for this person in this company doing this particular job. You explain that after meeting and talking to people in other companies, you feel that this is the finest company in the industry, and you want to work here.

If you've already received another job offer, be sure to mention it. This will increase your perceived value. You then explain to the decision-maker that based on your interview with him and based on your research, you feel that you can make the following specific contributions to his or her company. You say something like this: "I believe that I have some ideas by which this business or department can be greatly improved." Make it clear that you're not looking for a job and a paycheck; you are looking for an opportunity to perform and get results. Moreover, as a result of your job search, you have a pretty good idea of where you can make a valuable contribution to this organization. You can list the problems that you could solve for this employer and the benefits that they would enjoy from hiring you.

Explain how your experience, knowledge, and ability ideally qualify you to do this job the way you've described. Explain what hiring you would mean in terms of explicit advantages and benefits for the organization. Sell yourself based on your information and knowledge about the person, the company, and the industry.

A rule called the *universal hiring principle* says that you can create a job wherever you can convince the employer that they can make or save more money than the cost of hiring you. Companies always hire additional people as long as those people increase revenues or reduce costs in an amount greater than that of the salary and benefits paid. Demonstrate to the employer that this universal hiring principle applies to you. Remember, every job is an opportunity to solve problems or exploit opportunities. Wherever there are employers with problems unsolved or opportunities unexploited, there are job openings. Even in the midst of the worst depression in American history, fully 75 percent of the working population had jobs.

You can create a job wherever you can convince the employer that they can make or save more money than the cost of hiring you.

Through informational interviewing, you can ensure that you are fully employed for the rest of your life.

There are two other subjects of importance in the creative job search: preparing and using résumés, and how to conduct yourself to your greatest advantage in the interview.

The Function of Résumés

Everything we know about résumés suggests that no one is ever hired on the basis of a résumé. It is very much like a business card. It's something to be left rather than sent unless you have no other way to get it to the decision-maker.

If you're going to send a résumé, you should write an individual letter to a specific person with a one-page synopsis of your career attached. Do not send mass-produced or photocopied résumés. Especially, don't send letters to companies unless they are not addressed to a specific decision-maker whose name you've gotten by telephoning the organization or through some other channel.

There are two types of résumés: the chronological résumé, and the functional résumé. The chronological résumé lists your job accomplishments and credentials from the most recent job back to the beginning of your career. The functional résumé, on the other hand, organizes your work history in terms of the types of work you have done.

In both cases, the most important information to put in a résumé is an accurate description of your accomplishments and achievements in other positions. When a decision-maker looks at a résumé, he or she is looking for only one thing: transferability of results. The decision-maker is asking, what's in it for me? The answer in a résumé consists of specific accomplishments that may be transferable to this company. This is the only thing that causes a person to invite the sender of a résumé for an interview.

Don't have anyone else write a résumé for you. A professionally prepared résumé is obvious to the decision-maker and suggests that the individual does not have the intelligence or ability to write out a description of their own accomplishments without professional help.

It takes many résumés to generate an interview and many interviews to generate a job offer. Résumés are only a small part of a creative job search. As I've said, very few people are ever hired on the basis of a résumé. Most job decisions are made on the basis of the person, and often the résumé is not looked at all or only looked at afterwards.

The Job Interview

The most important thing about the job interview is appearing attractive and desirable to the interviewer. You must be dressed for success, well-groomed and with clothes that are appropriate for the job. A good rule is to dress as if you are going to the bank to apply for a loan with a weak financial statement. Be at your best in all respects. Always arrive ten minutes early for the interview. Many decision-makers will never hire a person who arrives late for a job interview, and I agree with that philosophy. It reflects a fundamental flaw in the person's character to come late to an interview, where they should be making the best first impression.

People will judge you in the first four seconds, and most professional interviewers agree that they have usually made a decision on the person within two minutes of beginning the interview. Your job is to be well-rested, positive, cheerful, and enthusiastic about the position. Your credentials are certainly important in the hiring decision, but when Burke, a marketing research company, did a survey of personnel executives, they found that the most influential keys to hiring decisions were the following ten factors:

1. Personality, or how you present yourself in the interview.
2. Experience or qualifications for the job; transferability of results.
3. Background and references: what other people will write and say about you.

4. Your enthusiasm about the potential employer and the possibility of getting the job.

5. Your educational and technical background.

6. Your growth potential: your ability to evolve and grow into a more valuable employee.

7. Your compatibility with the other types of people who work in the company.

8. Your intelligence and your capacity to learn, often indicated by the way you spend your personal time.

9. How the interviewer feels about you: how much he or she likes or trusts you.

10. How hard a worker you appear to be.

Higher-paid employees are selected differently. A second Burke survey indicated that a majority of top management executives agree on the following seven influencing factors in selecting a higher-paid person:

1. Personality and intelligence. Senior decision-makers feel that the right person with the right personality can compensate for a lack of specific job experience.

2. Aggressiveness and assertiveness in the job interview. Years of research have indicated that eagerness for the job is a good indication of how well the person will do on the job. By really wanting the job, you show how much you want to work in this company. But it's also a good idea to appear slightly nonchalant and make it clear that if you don't get the job, it won't kill you.

3. An interviewee who looks you straight in the eye as opposed to one who looks away.

4. Being fired from a previous job will not necessarily prevent you from being hired if that's the only thing you have going against you.

5. Being divorced is not a handicap in most hiring decisions.

6. Basic enthusiasm is one of the most important qualifications for most jobs, as well as a positive mental attitude and a cheerful personality.

7. Virtually all unsolicited letters written to top executives do get read, and most of them draw some response. If you write a personal letter directly to the decision-maker, in as many as 80 percent of cases they will read the letter and take some action on it. Between 2 and 10 percent of letters received in this way are acted upon favorably and can lead to an interview.

The creative job search is an ongoing process. Your duty to yourself is to get the kind of job that you can throw your whole heart and soul into. Insist on shopping and changing until you find a job you love, a job that you can lose yourself in. There are thousands of jobs available for the creative job seeker, but you must accept full responsibility for ensuring that you are working in the very best job for you at a place and in a company that utilizes your full range of talents and abilities, and which gives you ample opportunity to move upward and onward.

If you don't look forward to going to work, if you don't love what you're doing, if you don't enjoy the people you work with or the customers you sell to, you could well be in the wrong job and are in danger of wasting your working life.

Insist on working only at something you enjoy. Write out a description of your ideal job, and use the techniques of goal setting and strategic thinking to channel yourself into the position that will fill you with joy. Insisting upon working at something that you enjoy is an essential step to achieving financial independence. Otherwise you'll never really be happy or successful.

An Action Exercise

Here's an action exercise for you. Sit back and imagine that you could have any job you want. What would it be? If you could live and work anywhere you want, where would that be? If you could work with any kind of people, who would they be? Who has a job that you're a little envious of? What is he or she doing, and where is he or she working? Finally, what specific action step could you take this very minute to start working yourself into your dream job? Now it's up to you. Get started. Do something today.

Major Points

- Refuse to work at anything you don't enjoy.
- Begin your job search with a rigorous self-assessment.
- The informational interview is the core of successful job hunting.
- The most important thing about the job interview is appearing attractive to the interviewer.
- Get the kind of job that you can throw your whole heart and soul into.

ELEVEN

The Power of Leverage

In this chapter, we're going to talk about the forms of leverage that you can develop to accelerate your speed of advancement, multiply your results, and achieve financial independence. You're going to learn the well-known and not so well-known methods and techniques used by all highly successful men and women in our society. These techniques can dramatically increase the amount that you accomplish and the speed at which you accomplish it. The wonderful thing about them is that they're almost all free and require only self-discipline and persistent effort to incorporate them into your life.

There are basically ten types of leverage that you can develop to help yourself toward your goal of financial independence.

Knowledge

The first form of leverage is *knowledge*. Fully 70 percent of Americans today work in knowledge-based industries: the production, processing and distribution of various forms of knowledge. Being in the right place at the right time with a critical piece of knowledge can save you weeks, months, even years of hard work.

There's an old saying that knowledge is power. This isn't completely accurate. Only practical knowledge that can be applied to achieve some goal or benefit for yourself or someone else is power. Much knowledge is interesting and enjoyable but cannot be put to any practical use. Your job is to organize your life in such a way that you are continually seeking out and taking in new knowledge that you can use to move ahead more rapidly in your career. You can gain this knowledge through continuous study, as I've already mentioned. You can also gain knowledge by observing the activities of others. Successful men and women tend to be far more observant than the average. They tend to be highly aware of what's going on in their work and personal life, and they store their observations away for use later.

Seek new knowledge that you can use to move ahead more rapidly in your career.

You can gain knowledge by asking questions of knowledgeable people. Sometimes a few minutes spent with an expert will give you more practical knowledge than hours spent reading books and seeking information on your own.

Whenever you are not making progress because you lack a particular kind of knowledge, your first line of attack should be to see if you can find someone who's had the same problem and has the information to resolve it. Experts are usually open to talking to people who will ask questions and listen intently to the answers.

Leveraging Your Skill and Expertise

The second form of leverage is *skill* or *expertise*. People at the top are always paid far more than people who are just average. In sales, it's quite common for the top 20 percent of salespeople to make 80 percent of the sales and earn 80 percent of the commissions. This means that the top 20 percent of salespeople earn, on average, sixteen times the money of those in the bottom 80 percent.

In every field where the average sales income is $10,000 or $15,000 per year, there are men and women earning $300,000, $400,000, and $500,000 per year selling the same products or services at the same prices to the same people under the same competitive conditions. The difference is that the people in the top 20 percent have taken the time to develop the critical winning edges in their fields.

One salesman who came through our seminar was about to quit selling because he was being rejected nineteen times for every sale that he was making.

Instead of quitting, he decided to improve in two areas: prospecting, or finding qualified candidates, and closing sales.

By so doing, he improved his sales ratio from 1 in 20 to 1 in 15. Eventually, he lowered it to 1 in 10, then 1 in 5, then 1 in 3. By increasing his skills in prospecting and closing, he was able to double, triple, and finally quadruple his income in less than a year.

You can develop any skill you desire. There is endless information and training available in every field. All you have to do is go out, get the training, and put into practice what you learn.

You can develop any skill you desire.

Contacts and Networking

The third form of leverage is represented by your *contacts*: the people that you meet and network with. Your success will be in direct proportion to the number of people you know and who know you in a positive and favorable way. The more people you become acquainted with, the greater are the odds that you will meet the right person at the right time who will open the door of opportunity for you.

If you look back over your past life, you will find that almost every great opportunity or new direction came about as the result of meeting or knowing a particular person. Most self-made millionaires are excellent networkers. They are continually looking for opportunities to meet and interact with others who can help them and whom they can help in return.

Most self-made millionaires are excellent networkers.

One of the most powerful principles for success is the law of reciprocity. This law says that if you do something nice for another person, you will create within them an unconscious obligation or desire to pay you back and to do something nice for you.

There are many ways to network to your advantage. One is to join your trade or professional association and take an active part in its functions. At a stage in your career where you have more time than money, you should be out all the time, mixing with other people who can help you and whom you may be able to help in return.

If you're in sales, for example, join the organization called Sales & Marketing Executives International (SMEI). There's usually a branch in every large city. If you're in business, join your industry's professional or trade association. If you own your own business, join the Chamber of Commerce and perhaps a local service club such as the Rotary or the Lions Club.

When you join one of these organizations, look at the names and occupations of the members who serve on the boards and committees. Pick a board or committee that is important to the organization's success and has members it might be helpful for you to know. Volunteer for work on that committee. Accept responsibility and take charge. Develop a reputation for making a valuable contribution. Volunteer for additional assignments. Get yourself known by attending every committee meeting and participating in every weekly or monthly general meeting. Don't push yourself on others, but remember what Woody Allen said: "80 percent of success is just showing up." This form of networking brings you to the attention of men and women who may be in a position to help you, and it does so in a nonthreatening way. It gives you an opportunity to show your stuff, to demonstrate to others what you're made of, without ever asking them for anything.

Volunteering is an excellent way to demonstrate your skills in the job market.

Another excellent career move is to get involved with community services and activities that you believe in and care about. My entire career was changed by getting actively involved in the United Way. It brought me into contact with the leading businesspeople of the community and eventually resulted in my doing more business in three months than I had done in the previous three years. This came about because I was willing to contribute my time and energies to a worthwhile charity at no charge. My activities got me tremendous exposure to many people who eventually became my clients and customers.

Another way to build your contacts and relationships is to write out a strategic plan to meet the top 100 men and women in your community. As you read the local newspapers and magazines, as you talk to people and hear the names of men and women who are the movers and shakers in your community, write their names down. Then plan to write them a letter. Get involved in their community-supported activities or political party or find some way to attend functions or network with people who know them. Do you think it would be helpful to you to know and be known by the top 100 people in your community? You bet it would.

Leveraging Money

The fourth form of leverage that can help you move ahead faster is *money*. Money is terribly important for several reasons. The first is that when you have money in the bank, you're a very different person in your relationships with others than if you have no money and you're tense about your bills and debts. Accumulating money improves your character and makes you a stronger and more self-confident person. It makes you more effective and persuasive with others.

A second reason that money is important is that having it enables you to take advantage of opportunities that come along. If the best opportunity to increase your net worth were to get in on the ground floor of a new business selling a popular product or service but you had no money to invest, it would do you no good.

As I travel around the country, I meet countless men and women who have been presented with wonderful opportunities but could do nothing with them because they had no savings. They've gotten into the habit of spending everything they earn and a little bit more besides, so they are trapped on an endless treadmill of debt and repayment.

A third reason for accumulating money is so that you can walk away from a bad job. The fastest way to boost your income is to quit and get a better job that pays more somewhere else. You are only as free as your options. You are only free when there is something else you can do and somewhere else you can go. It is a waste of life is to have to stay at a job that you don't like. Probably 80 percent of Americans working today are caught in these golden chains. They cannot leave their jobs because of their debts and bills.

The fastest way to boost your income is to quit and get a better job that pays more somewhere else.

Good Work Habits

The fifth form of leverage that you can develop is *good work habits*: the ability to get the job done in a quality fashion. In a study of 104 chief executive officers, they were asked to identify the qualities that would most mark a young person for rapid promotion. Eighty-five percent of them agreed that two qualities were more important than anything else: the ability to separate the relevant from the irrelevant, the ability to set priorities, and the ability to get a job done fast without delay. As we've seen, the person with good work habits is the one who works all the time they are at work. This person will get a reputation for working harder than their peers and colleagues. Probably nothing will bring you to the attention of your superiors faster than getting a reputation for being the person who works harder than anyone else.

High Energy

The sixth form of leverage that you can develop is *high energy*. To get ahead of the others, you must have the stamina and energy to work longer and harder than they do. It's often said that in America, you work forty hours per week for survival, and everything over that is for success. If you're only working forty hours a week, you're merely treading water, staying even with bills and expenses. To get ahead, you have to increase your average workweek from forty to fifty or even sixty hours—the average workweek of the executive or entrepreneur.

Some years ago, the retiring president of the American Chamber of Commerce shared his secret for lifelong success at his farewell banquet. He said he had learned it as a young man. It was contained in a quote stuck to his school bulletin board. It said, "Your success in life will be in direct proportion to what you do *after* you do what you're expected to do." He used this as his guiding principle, and it made him one of the most respected and successful men in America.

After a lifetime of studying men and women who rose from poverty to wealth, Napoleon Hill concluded that going the extra mile was the single habit that had opened the doors of opportunity for them. Always doing more than you're paid for, putting in more hours than are expected, is the key to rapid advancement. The Red Sea of opportunity seems to open up before the person who is willing to give more of himself or herself than the average.

Doing more than you're paid for is the key to rapid advancement.

In order to go the extra mile, you must have extra strength, energy, and vitality. Build up your energy by sleeping seven or eight hours a night, eating the right foods in the right combinations, and getting regular exercise. Every practice that gives you greater energy and vitality is an investment in your present and your future.

Personality and Communication

The seventh form of leverage is a *positive personality* combined with good *communication skills.* Perhaps the fastest way to get ahead in America is to be a likable, cheerful, and optimistic person whom other people enjoy being around. Liking is one of the most powerful factors for influencing people to cooperate with you. When people like you, they'll want to do business with you, buy from you, lend you money, give you the benefit of the doubt, and promote and advance you faster than they otherwise would.

Having good communication skills means not only speaking well but having a good vocabulary. You can't hide your command of the English language. Many studies demonstrate that your level of income is closely correlated to the number of words that you can use and recognize when you communicate. The minute you open your mouth, you are immediately pigeonholed by the people around you.

Having good communication skills means not only speaking well but having a good vocabulary.

Many decent, talented, and hardworking men and women are passed over for jobs and promotions because their use of the English language is poor. Each new word that you learn is connected to as many as ten other words. If you make a habit of learning one new word per day, you will learn 365 new words per year. If these words are each connected to or associated with ten others, you will have learned to recognize and use as many as 3,650 new words in a year. Since the average American uses less than 2,000 words in their entire vocabulary, you can have a vocabulary that ranks you among the top 10 percent of the population.

Vocabulary is also important in that words are the tools of thought. The more words that you know, the more skillful a thinker you will become. A larger vocabulary enables you to think and speak with greater clarity and accuracy and allows you to understand and deal with more complex issues and ideas.

As you develop a broader vocabulary, you should also think of learning how to speak on your feet. Join your local chapter of Toastmasters International. In six months, you can overcome your fears of public speaking and be able to give a competent public talk on a few minutes' notice. You can also take a course from Dale Carnegie Training to build self-confidence, communication skills, and the ability to speak effectively in front of others.

Perhaps no other investment in yourself will pay off more than learning how to be an effective and skilled communicator in front of an audience. Salespeople who are held back because of their fears of rejection have found that a course in public speaking dramatically increases their self-confidence in prospecting and cold calling. They rapidly see the results of this new self-confidence in bigger paychecks and larger commissions. The development of excellent communication skills and a broader vocabulary is an investment in time that will pay off in success.

A Positive Image

The eighth form of leverage that you can develop is a *positive, successful image*. People judge you by the way you look on the outside. Fully 95 percent of the first impression that you make on others is determined by the clothes you wear, if only because they cover 95 percent of your body.

Some people think it's not right for others to judge them by their clothes or appearance. This is simply self-delusion. You judge and categorize everybody else by the way they look, and that is the way that they judge you.

The best way to deal with this phenomenon is to accept that your appearance and image will have an inordinate impact on the way you are viewed by others. It will certainly affect the kind of job you get, how often you're promoted, the money you're paid, and the way you're treated by your boss, coworkers, and subordinates. At the very minimum, read John Malloy's book *Dress for Success* (there are separate volumes for men and women).

Ideally, you should dress for two positions above your current job. In other words, you should dress the way your boss's boss dresses. It's been proved over and over that people like to work with, promote, and pay people who dress and look like themselves or better.

Don't make the mistake of taking your cues for dress from fashion magazines. Their articles on clothing and style are written in order to sell the advertising on the accompanying pages. Their recommendations for acceptable business dress are almost invariably wrong. If you believe that it's OK to lighten up and dress casually because you read it in a magazine, you may find yourself overlooked for promotion or not even hired in the first place.

Take your cues from the successful men and women around you. Look at the way that the top executives in your company where you work are dressing. And look at the way that the top people whose pictures appear in the newspapers and magazines are dressing. If you're going to be a follower in fashion, follow the leaders, not the followers, and certainly not the fashion magazines.

Character

The ninth form of leverage that will exert a tremendous influence on your success in America is your *character*. As Ralph Waldo Emerson said, "What you do speaks so loudly I cannot hear what you are saying." Your character is the sum total result of your values, self-discipline, morals, and especially your integrity.

Your character is the sum total result of your values, self-discipline, morals, and integrity.

I've served as a consultant to hundreds of corporations over the years. In virtually every case, I found the men and women in positions of responsibility to possess the highest character and integrity. Men and women with character tend to move up into positions of authority within every organization of value.

Your character will be partly determined by your dependability, by whether or not you do what you say you will do. It will also be judged partly on your level of determination, on how badly you want a particular job. As much as anything, your character will be judged by the way that you treat other people. As Thomas Carlyle said, you can tell a big man by the way he treats little men.

You cannot fake character, but you can develop it by deciding on your basic values and living in a manner that is consistent with them, never compromising them for anything. The more you exert self-discipline and self-control, the stronger and finer your character will be.

Others can easily read your character—the sum total of what you are. A fine character can go a long way to moving you up the ladder of success, whereas a serious character flaw, such as dishonesty or unreliability, can be fatal to your success.

Luck

The tenth form of leverage enjoyed by all successful people in America is *luck*.

It's amazing how many successful men and women ascribe much of their success to luck. However, we know that in a perfect universe, governed by law, there are no accidents. Luck is simply a way of explaining events that the person doesn't understand. What seems to be luck is merely a demonstration of the iron law of cause and effect, especially the law of attraction. You attract into your life people, ideas, circumstances, and opportunities that are in harmony with your dominant thoughts and character.

When you increase your store of practical knowledge, you trigger the law of attraction. When you upgrade your skills, you attract more opportunities to use those skills. When you increase your number of contacts, you tend to attract the people who can help you get the things you want. When you save money, you again trigger the law of attraction, which brings more money and more opportunities to use it. When you develop good work habits, you attract opportunities to apply them toward getting more and more important things done. When you discipline yourself to eat, sleep, and exercise for high levels of health and vitality, you attract opportunities to apply your energies to productive purposes. When you develop good communication skills and a positive personality, you attract into your life other positive, people who can help you and whom you can help in return. When you develop character based on a high code of moral principles, you attract into your life people of the same caliber, who will work with you toward the achievement of your objectives.

When you do all of these things, you begin to have what other people call luck. You have a remarkable series of experiences that seem to speed you along the road toward your innermost desires and aspirations.

An Action Exercise

Here's an action exercise for you. Make a list of the ten forms of leverage:

Knowledge	High energy
Skill	Positive image
Contacts	Positive personality
Money	Character
Good work habits	Luck

Write these down the left-hand side of a page, with three lines between each one. Then write out at least three specific actions you could take to begin developing each form of leverage in your life. Select the most obvious one in each category and get started now.

The Right Boss

One key for getting onto the fast track is to work for the right company and the right boss. The right company is one that respects its people and practices pay for performance. It is dynamic, growing, open to new ideas, and full of opportunities for people with ambition and initiative.

It's important to pick your boss carefully and refuse to work for a difficult, negative person. Much of your happiness and job satisfaction depends upon your relationship with your superior. If you don't get along with him or her, make every effort to resolve the situation or get transferred. If you can't, be prepared to walk away. Choosing the right work, the right place to do it, and the right people to do it with lays the foundation for success.

The Niche Strategy

Once you've established superior work habits and found the right context to grow professionally, you are ready to implement the niche strategy. It is based on the fact that some jobs are more critical to the health of the organization than others.

A strategic niche is a job or position that influences the cash flow of the company. In most companies, cash flow is determined by sales and marketing. In the 1960s, Buck Rodgers (not the science fiction hero) became one of the most powerful people in IBM because he was in charge of marketing—the lifeblood of the company.

If you want to get ahead rapidly in most companies, you must work your way into the sales and marketing functions. Many people at my seminars ask me how they can make more money at their jobs. When they tell me their positions, the problem is usually clear: they're working in areas and at jobs that are felt to be of lesser importance. As a result, their services are not as highly valued, no matter how hard they work or how well they do their job. Their increases are set at a level that will keep them from quitting or will enable the company to hire someone else quickly if they do quit. They are stuck where they are.

To increase your income, you must be in a position to increase the company's income, to increase revenues or reduce expenses. Look at your company and look for that niche where you can become more valuable. Once you make yourself valuable, then go the extra mile and make yourself indispensable.

Many companies are reluctant to pay their salespeople too much. They feel that no one should earn as much as the senior executives. If you're in such a position and you want to earn what you are worth, you have no choice but to begin looking around for a company that will pay you based on performance rather than on politics and the ego needs of the senior executives. If your job involves working for another company, no matter what your position, you owe it to yourself to continually seek ways to move upward faster. Your job is to earn the very highest return on your energy, the highest return on your ability to work and produce results.

If you face such hurdles in your organization and cannot move up as quickly as you want, the best strategy is to quit and start your own business. Fully 74 percent of self-made millionaires in America achieve their wealth by starting and building their own businesses.

Ten Ways to Get Ahead

Here are ten great rules for getting ahead in your career.

1. Develop staying power. Make a commitment to your job and your career. Make it clear to your boss that you're there for the long term, that you are committed to the success of your organization, and that you are a dedicated and loyal employee.

2. Never use your family or your extracurricular activities as an excuse for not giving 100 percent to your work. This is a sign of weakness and causes your superiors to suspect your long-term intentions.

3. Put in more time than anyone else. Get there a little bit earlier, work a little bit harder, and stay a little bit later. There is nothing more impressive to a boss than to see you there when they arrive and see you there when they depart. Putting in an extra thirty or sixty minutes per day can have a major impact on how fast you move ahead.

4. Network with other people for information, counsel, advice, and guidance. Your ability to network and interact effectively with people inside and outside your company could be the most important thing you do. Don't waste your lunch hours and evenings in idle socializing. Put those hours to work by spending time around people who can help you and whom you can help in return.

5. Specialize, and develop a valuable area of expertise. Make yourself important, and then make yourself indispensable.

6. Learn how to be a manager. Inspect what you expect. Take full responsibility for results and refuse to make any excuses. If things go wrong, move fast when there's a crisis.

7. Be a team player. Support and cooperate with others. The way you are known to your coworkers will have a major impact on whether or not you are promoted.

8. Thank those who help you. Express appreciation in the form of thank you notes and little gestures. Whenever you thank someone, you make them feel good about themselves. You then create within them a desire to earn your thanks so that they can feel good about themselves again.

9. Use your appearance to create an image of strength and credibility. Dress professionally from head to toe. Always look, walk, talk, and act the part of the successful person that you intend to be.

10. Be loyal to your boss, your company, your department, and your coworkers. Never say anything to anyone inside or outside the company that can be construed as critical or disloyal. This form of disloyalty, of speaking badly of someone, especially your boss, can do more to sabotage your career in an organization than anything that you can dream of.

Here's an important rule for success: everybody knows everything. Never for a moment should you think that anything that you say to another person will remain a secret for long. If you don't want something that you say to be relayed back to the worst possible person who could hear it, then don't say it at all.

Your operating principle for politics and communications within your organization must be that everybody knows everything. Accepting this as a firm rule will save you an enormous amount of time, trouble, and explanations in the future.

Remember also that your most important customer is your boss. You have been hired to please your boss. This is neither good nor bad; it's merely a fact. You and I make our livings from customer satisfaction. We are all paid in direct proportion to how well we satisfy our customers, whoever they may be. Your number one customer in your career is the person who has put you into your position. Many people feel that their bosses are simply necessary evils to be worked around and put up with. However, fast-trackers realize that their career is attached to the boss and how much they satisfy the boss on an ongoing basis.

The essence of getting and keeping your career on the fast track is to see yourself as self-employed. The top 3 percent of men and women in every industry are those who act as if they own the place. When they refer to the company, they use words such as *we* and *us*, *our* and *my*. They look upon everything that happens in the company as personally affecting them. They're emotionally involved in what they do, and they're committed to the success of the organization. When your boss sees that you are determined to get ahead by helping him or her achieve his or her goals and accepting full responsibility for the survival and growth of the organization, you will move onto the fast track and into position for higher pay and greater responsibilities.

One last point: When you make all of these efforts and begin to enjoy the rewards, you will find that it's not very crowded on the fast track. Most people are simply not willing to make the extra efforts necessary to stand out. They've been given wrong information, and they've reached wrong conclusions. They believe that the best way to work is to do as little as you can get away with.

When you redefine the terms of the competition, you will move out in front of the pack onto the fast track. You will be on your way to earning the kind of money you desire and deserve. You'll be on the way toward achieving financial independence during your working lifetime.

Major Points

- You can develop any skill you desire.
- Your success will be in direct proportion to what you do after you do what you're expected to do.
- Learn how to be an effective communicator in front of an audience.
- You attract people, ideas, and opportunities that are in harmony with your dominant thoughts and character.
- You cannot fake character.
- Work for the right company and the right boss.
- Use the niche strategy to advance.

TWELVE

Achieve Financial Independence

Perhaps your most important responsibility is to achieve financial independence for yourself and your family. Aside from the tangible benefits of having all the money you need, there are even more important reasons for obtaining financial freedom. I've already talked about the law of control, which says that you feel good about yourself to the degree to which you feel you are in control of your own life. Perhaps no single factor will rob you of a sense of control more than feeling that you don't have enough money to pay your bills or support your lifestyle.

Your most important responsibility is to achieve financial independence for yourself and your family.

The most basic human need is for security, including the freedom from fear of poverty. The fear of poverty and the fear of failure associated with it causes more unhappiness and underachievement than perhaps any other single factor. Achieving financial independence is the critical issue in whether you become everything you're capable of becoming. People who are worried about money all the time never have a chance to enjoy the finer things of life.

Financial independence begins with a state of mind. Wealth starts with a goal accompanied by affirmations, visualization, and emotionalization. These are to be repeated until the goal is driven deep into your subconscious mind, where it activates all the mental laws that I've already discussed.

Financial freedom is only possible when you accept complete responsibility for your financial condition and you refuse to make excuses. Accepting personal responsibility for everything that you accomplish comes before any meaningful improvement can take place.

Financial freedom is only possible when you accept complete responsibility for your financial condition.

The inability to delay gratification is the chief reason people worry about money all their lives and retire poor. The inability to refrain from spending everything you make, and a little bit more besides, will guarantee that you will worry endlessly about money. Conversely, the ability to delay gratification, to refrain from spending in the short term so that you can enjoy financial independence in the long term, is the chief reason people achieve such independence.

The law of accumulation says that every great achievement is an accumulation of hundreds, if not thousands, of little efforts and sacrifices that no one ever sees or appreciates. A great career is preceded by thousands of hours of hard work and preparation for excellence.

Financial independence is also preceded by small efforts of saving and sacrifice, repeated hundreds, perhaps thousands, of times with the knowledge that these efforts will eventually accumulate a large amount of money. This will enable you to retire wealthy and never have to worry about money again.

The law of attraction says that like attracts like. You've heard it said that it takes money to make money. When you begin to put a little money aside, it begins to radiate a magnetic energy that starts to attract more money to you. As long as your attitude towards your money is positive and respectful, you'll acquire more and more of it. As you increase your savings and invest your positive emotions in them, more and more money will be attracted to you from a variety of unexpected sources. The more you have, the stronger the magnetic force will be, and the more will come to you.

On the other hand, the less money you have—and especially if you have none—the less magnetic force there is attracting money into your life, and you'll have money problems all the time. The starting point of financial independence is to save part of your income every single month.

The basic rule for financial accumulation has always been to pay yourself first. Each time you get your paycheck, take a certain amount off the top and put it into an account for financial accumulation. Never touch this money, except for careful, conservative investment. Most people do what is fatal to financial success: they only save what is left over after they've paid all their bills and expenses. But to achieve financial independence, you must pay your expenses with what is left over after you've saved a minimum amount from each paycheck.

Pay yourself first.

Your minimum target amount for monthly savings is 10 percent of your net income. If your net income is $10,000 per month after all taxes and deductions, then you would place $1,000 into a savings account each month before you began paying for other things. You must begin to train yourself to live on 90 percent of your net income.

What If You're in Debt?

What if you're in debt when you begin? What if you don't have enough money to last out the month as it is? Then begin by saving whatever you can. With a little effort, you can easily save1 or 2 percent of your net income. You can live on the other 98 or 99 percent. As you become comfortable with living on 98 percent, you can increase your savings to 3 or 4 percent per month, and then later to 5 or 6 percent until you eventually get it up to 10 percent per month.

In the meantime, cut down on all unnecessary expenses and commit a minimum percentage of your income each month to reducing your debt. Now you'll have two accounts: one for financial accumulation and one for debt reduction. In a short time, you'll become accustomed to living on 98 percent of your income, then 95 percent, then 90 percent, then eventually 85 percent, 80 percent, and so on.

W. Clement Stone put it very well when he wrote, "If you cannot save money, then the seeds of greatness are not in you." Your blueprint for financial independence begins with disciplining yourself to live on less than you earn, and eventually to live on a good deal less than you earn.

The major psychological benefit of saving money is that it gives you a tremendous feeling of self-respect and self-esteem. A person who has money in the bank and in their pocket is very different from one who has no savings and who is totally preoccupied with money worries.

To become wealthy, you must fight against the almost irresistible power of Parkinson's law, which says that expenditures always rise to meet income. No matter how much you earn, your cost of living tends to rise to absorb every extra penny. If your income moves up from $4,000 per month to $10,000 per month, if you're not extremely well disciplined, you'll find that your cost of living will rise to the same level and will absorb everything that you're making.

Thomas Stanley, author of *The Millionaire Next Door*, studied thousands of affluent Americans. He concluded there are two types of people: those who look as if they have a lot of money, and then those who really do. His studies concluded that people who seem to be doing extremely well—driving flashy cars, taking expensive vacation, buying lots of expensive clothes—are usually living just one paycheck ahead of the bill collectors. Wealthy people, including most self-made millionaires, live on ordinary streets, drive ordinary cars, and live ordinary lifestyles. One example was the late Sam Walton of Walmart stores, then the richest man in America. In 1988, when he was worth $8.7 billion, Sam Walton was still driving to work in a pickup truck. Many wealthy men and women drive ordinary cars, because most of their money is busy working for them somewhere else. Many people who look wealthy have all their money invested in symbols of wealth, which are losing value every day.

The Three Legs of Financial Planning

The three legs of the financial planning stool are *savings, insurance,* and *investments.* With regard to savings, your philosophy should be to build a financial fortress: an amount of money that protects you from the unexpected ups and downs of a dynamic economy. Your minimum goal for savings should be to have between two and six months of living expenses put aside in a fairly liquid form, such as savings accounts, money market accounts, or a money market mutual fund.

Build a financial fortress: an amount of money that protects you from the unexpected ups and downs of the economy.

When you've built your financial fortress, you'll have become a totally different person. You'll have an aura of unshakable self-confidence and self-assurance. You won't have to put up with a job or a boss that you don't like, nor will you have to stay working at something simply because you can't afford to quit. You'll be able to do what is best for you. You'll be able to choose the work you want to do and the people you want to work with. You'll be able to choose only to do what you love to do rather than being forced to do work that has no meaning for you aside from the paycheck.

The second part of financial planning is *life insurance.* You should only buy life insurance if you have a family to provide for. The only kind of life insurance that you should buy is *term insurance,* which is much cheaper than any other kind. You can buy it in almost any amount, and it will pay out the face value of the policy to your estate or your family should you die.

When you become wealthy and have an estate that you need to protect from estate duties upon your death, you can think about permanent insurance, which has an equity or cash buildup contained in the premium and which can never be canceled for any reason. Until that point, you should only buy term insurance, and only if you have a family to support.

Buy enough term insurance so that its proceeds will enable your family to maintain its current standard of living. If your current income is $100,000 per year and your family could earn 10 percent per annum off the proceeds from a life insurance policy, you should have $1 million worth of term insurance, payable to your spouse as your beneficiary. In the event of your death, this amount would go directly to your spouse, and it would go tax-free.

The third leg of the financial planning stool is *investment*. Investments will eventually make you wealthy, and it's absolutely essential that you become as wise as a serpent and as clever as a fox in investing your money.

Investing

The first investment that you should take maximum advantage of is a self-directed, tax-sheltered investment such as an IRA, a Keogh plan, or if possible a company pension plan. Even though the amount you can put into these plans is limited, you should take advantage of them and invest every single possible cent that you're allowed to put into them. Money that accumulates in a tax-sheltered plan can grow at a rate of 50 to 100 percent faster than money invested outside of such a plan, which is subject to taxation. Your earnings in the form of interest and dividends are fully taxable if they are outside of an

IRA or Keogh plan. The earnings in an IRA or Keogh Plan are tax-deferred: they continue to grow and compound without taxes until you actually take them out of the plan when you retire.

Once you've taken maximum advantage of tax-sheltered investments, you should consider three other types of investments.

The first is a money market fund. A money market fund is different from a money market account at your bank in that it is invested more aggressively and pays a higher rate of interest. Money market funds can be opened for as little as $500, and they're available from almost all financial planning organizations. When you put your money into a money market fund, it's very important to read its prospectus and make sure that the costs of administration of the fund are no more than 0.5 or 0.75 percent per year. If they're in excess of that amount, you should seek another fund.

The time to invest in money market funds is when interest rates or the stock market seem to be unstable and unpredictable. The ideal time to invest in a money market fund is when interest rates are rising and especially if the prime lending rate—the rate at which the Federal Reserve lends money to banks—is high. That's the time when you'll get your highest and safest return on your savings in a money market fund.

The second investment that you can use is a *stock mutual fund*. The only kind of mutual fund for you to consider is a *no-load fund*. A no-load fund charges you no commissions for investing: 100 percent of the amount that you put in goes to work for you immediately. A full-load mutual fund will charge you as much as 8.5 or 9 percent commission for the privilege of investing your hard-earned money. That money will be paid to the person who has sold you the investment. It will not be deposited to your account, nor will it be available to you ever again. If you pay this kind of a commission, your investment will have to grow by 8.5 to 9 percent just to enable you to get back to even. Yet there's very little difference in financial performance between a no-load mutual fund and a full-load mutual fund.

The only kind of mutual fund you should consider is a no-load fund.

Several organizations offer no-load mutual funds. You can find advertisements for them online, in financial periodicals, and in mutual fund guides. You can ask around and get advice from other people you know who are using them.

The first rule of investment is always to investigate before you invest. The only thing that is easy about money is losing it. Making money requires patience, fortitude, and never-ending vigilance even in mutual funds. The time to invest in a stock-based mutual fund is when the prime interest rate is declining. The rise and fall of the prime rate correlates closely with economic expansion and recession, with booms and busts in the stock market. When interest rates are low, the cost of capital is low, and therefore businesses rush to invest and increase their productive capacity and their profits. When interest rates are high, companies cut back on their numbers of workers and decrease their activities.

A stock mutual fund is invested in by thousands of individual investors like you. This pool of funds is invested in a broad cross-section of stocks traded on the major stock markets of the United States or other countries. A mutual fund is managed by professional money managers: people who watch the market full-time. These professionals have available to them enormous quantities of information that individual investors simply do not have access to.

Since a mutual fund invests in a broad selection of stocks, your risk is spread over a broad range. Many well-managed mutual funds increase in value greatly in excess of the general market. When the market slumps, most mutual funds do not decline as much as the overall market averages or individual stocks. A no-load mutual fund, professionally managed in a broad assortment of carefully selected stocks, is one of the best investments for financial growth.

The third type of investment is *no-load bond mutual funds*. The best time to invest in a bond fund is when interest rates have peaked and are declining. At this point, the value of the individual shares in the bond fund increases. Since bond funds are composed of securities with fixed rates of return, as the average interest rate in the marketplace declines, the return on these bonds, relatively speaking, goes up.

Let me explain. Let's say that you buy a single bond with a $1,000 face value, and it pays 10 percent interest per annum. Your return will be $100 per annum. Now let's say that the prime interest rate drops to 8 percent: 8 percent now becomes the multiple at which people will buy bonds. New bonds will be issued at 8 percent, and outstanding bonds that are paying 10 percent will increase in value, to about $1,200 per $1,000 in face amount. By paying $1,200 for the bond, the return to the investor will be 8 percent. This is why you buy bonds when market interest rates are declining; every point of decline in the prime rate increases the value of the bond fund by as much as 10 percent.

To summarize, the best investment vehicles for financial accumulation for the average person are no-load mutual funds, either a stock fund, a bond fund, or a money market fund.

The Best Single Investment?

What is the best single investment? There's no answer to this question. At one point in the economy, one investment will be better than the others. As the economy and interest rates change, another investment will be better. Watch your investments carefully, and take 100 percent responsibility for every decision you make about allocating your funds; no one else can make your decisions for you.

One successful businessman was asked about the philosophy that had enabled him to acquire so many companies and so much money. He said that he had just two rules. Rule number one was, "Don't lose money." Rule number two was, "Whenever you are tempted, refer back to rule number one." A Japanese proverb says that making money is like digging sand with a pin, whereas losing money is like pouring water into the sand.

Money is hard to earn and easy to lose. If all you did throughout the course of your working lifetime was to save 10 percent or more of your income and put it away, letting it accumulate at interest, that alone would make you financially independent. When you lose money, you are also losing the number of months and years that it took you to accumulate that money. You're actually losing a part of your life—the amount of your life that you had to exchange for the amount of money that you lost. Whenever someone reaches the point of feeling they can afford to lose a little money in an investment, you can be sure of one thing: that person is going to lose not only a little but probably a lot of money. Your attitude must always be, don't lose money.

All serious money in the United States is conservative money. It is what economists call *risk-averse money*. Serious people with serious money continually seek for ways to increase their money by minimizing risk, not by seeking risk. Successful entrepreneurs and businesspeople are not risk takers. The successful ones are risk avoiders. That's how they became successful.

A basic rule for investment is to spend at least as much time in investigating an investment as you spent earning the money you're investing. Nothing takes the place of research. Many financial advisors who are selling various investments are not particularly well off themselves, and they often know very little about what they're recommending.

Spend at least as much time in investigating an investment as you spent earning the money you're investing.

Your attitude toward financial accumulation should be that when you put the money aside, you never spend it, not for any reason. You don't put the money aside for a rainy day. You don't save up so that you can buy a motor home or a boat. You set up different accounts for those things. Your savings and investment funds are put away, never to be touched, to grow and multiply over the course of the years until they yield you the financial independence you desire.

Wealthy men and women in America have low debt or no debt. The only kind of debt that they allow is debt for investments into assets that are paying back more than the cost of money they've borrowed. The only kind of real estate they own is real estate whose mortgages and all expenses are serviced by the rent that comes from the real estate. The only time they've borrowed to invest in their companies is when they can earn a higher rate of return in their companies than they have to pay for the money in the first place.

If you want to enjoy peace of mind and become financially independent, make a plan, starting today, to pay off all your debts and live debt-free, aside from your home mortgage and perhaps your car. Never borrow for food, rent, transportation, clothes, or other things that you use on a monthly and yearly basis. You should lease or rent assets that depreciate or lose value, and you should only borrow to invest in assets that go up in value as time passes in excess of the cost of the money or the interest rate.

Three Periods of Life

You have three periods in your life with regard to money. The first twenty-five years are your *learning years*. During this time, you acquire your basic education, your basic ability to earn money.

The next forty years are called your *earning years*. These are the years when you work the hardest and increase your income the most.

The last twenty years are called your *yearning years*. These are the years when you look forward to retirement, either a comfortable one or one accompanied by financial worries.

Most people make the greatest amount of money in their lives after the age of forty-five. After this age, your expenses for raising your family begin to diminish (in most cases), and you're being paid the highest amounts that you've ever earned. During this time, you can begin to save 20, 30, and even 40 percent of your income to run up your savings and investment accounts to their maximum prior to retirement.

Even if you are in your late teens or early twenties, for the sake of your character, your peace of mind, and your future, you must begin to save and put money aside. People who say silly things such as, "I'm not here for a long time; I'm here for a good time" have a failure attitude and will be in serious financial trouble before their careers are over.

Wealth can be defined as simply *cash flow from other sources*. You're only wealthy to the degree to which you do not have to go to work each day to support your standard of living. Wealthy people can stop working with no interruption in their lifestyles.

Your primary job during your financial accumulation years is to build up a portfolio of assets that yield you an income that will eventually be greater than the income that you earn from working. At that point, you can stop working if you desire and spend more of your time managing your investments.

What Not to Invest In

Never invest in gold, silver, or precious metals. Gold gives you no rate of return. It is inert. Many people make a lot of money by selling gold, silver, and precious metals, but the people who purchase them seldom make anything.

In addition, never purchase an investment over the phone, unless it's from a known and respected company. The United States today is full of confidence games and scams being sold over the phone to unsuspecting investors. These people often work out of motels and bucket shops, and they move from place to place as soon as the police become aware of them. Their favorite swindles are in commodities, precious metals, and penny stocks. If someone calls you to offer any one of these, hang up so fast that it makes their ears burn. I have met so many people who have lost so much money and so many years of hard work to these swindles that it almost breaks my heart. Don't be one of them.

Don't invest in antiques, oriental carpets, coins, or stamps unless you're a full-time expert in those fields. On any given day, as many of those investments are decreasing in value as increasing. Fully 90 percent of all original artworks, such as paintings sculptures, never see their initial retail sales price again. From the time you purchase them, they decline in value usually by 80 percent or more. These are not good investments for a person who is serious about becoming rich. You buy these things only when you are already wealthy, and then you buy them for their beauty and the pleasure they give you, but not as an investment.

Don't invest in oil, gas, or mining stocks. Don't invest in commodities, even with reputable commodity dealers. Commodities are the most dangerous and volatile of all investments; virtually everyone who invests in them for any period of time loses almost everything that they put in.

An Action Exercise

Here's an exercise for you. Sit down and write out a plan for financial accumulation. Head a series of milestones or goals for one, two, three, four, and five. Launch your plan by reaching into your pocket and put it as much as you can into a jar or piggy bank. Open a wealth building savings account and put something into it from every paycheck.

Finally, put yourself on a budget. Make a habit of writing down in a small notebook every penny you spend daily. Each week, take some time to review your expenditures with a view toward reducing consumption and increasing savings. If you can discipline yourself to do all of this, if you can delay gratification, you'll be well on the way to financial freedom and to the peace of mind that you desire.

Major Points

- Your most important responsibility is to achieve financial independence.
- The key to prosperity is the ability to delay gratification.
- Pay yourself first.
- Your minimum target amount for monthly savings is 10 percent of your net income.
- Fight Parkinson's law, which says that expenditures always rise to meet income.
- The three legs of financial planning are savings, insurance, and investments.
- Put yourself on a budget.

Afterword

We've been on a long journey together. We've explored how to take charge of your life and achieve success and fulfillment. We started with the importance of values, then went on to goals and plans. We've explored how to make use of the superconscious mind—the greatest power in the universe—to enrich our lives and those of others. We've gone through the process of discovering the ideal career and how to develop it. Finally, we explained financial independence and how to achieve it.

One last point remains, and I have held it for last because of its extreme importance: the central role of service in achieving personal greatness. The need for meaning and purpose is often the greatest single need of the human being. Men and women will die for a sense of meaning and purpose in their lives. If we achieve all kinds of monetary rewards, but we have no sense of purpose, our external accomplishments will give us no lasting satisfaction.

We are structured in such a way that we achieve meaning and purpose in our lives by *transcendence*—rising above the tangible, material elements of our lives. To achieve transcendence, we must commit ourselves to something bigger and higher than ourselves. The only way to achieve transcendence is by losing ourselves in service to some great cause. The only great cause that can motivate you continuously is something that has to do with uplifting, enhancing, and improving the lives of others.

Human beings can be characterized as lazy, greedy, ambitious, selfish, vain, ignorant, and impatient. There is much truth to this description. Yet we are also designed in such a way that we can never really achieve pleasure from any accomplishments unless we feel that we're making a contribution to humankind. All great men and women have felt that in some way their lives belong not to themselves, but to humanity at large. They had a sense of destiny; they felt that they were put on this earth to do something special to help and uplift the lives of others.

I've stressed that the one central point of success is determining a definite major goal for yourself. There are many goals you can choose, but I'm convinced that for this goal to be successful, it must include *service*—helping other human beings in some way. If you can integrate this truth into your aspirations and efforts, not only will you succeed, but your success will benefit the entire human race.